Crisis

A Guide for Ministering to People in Crisis

Roslyn A. Karaban, PhD

Caring

Resource Publications

San Jose, California

Reprint Department
Resource Publications, Inc.
160 E. Virginia St. #290
San Jose, CA 95112-5876
(408) 286-8505
(408) 287-8748 fax

Library of Congress Cataloging-in-Publication Data

Karaban, Roslyn A.
    Crisis caring : a guide for ministering to people in crisis / Roslyn A. Karaban.
        p. cm.
    Includes bibliographical references.
    ISBN 0-89390-612-3
    1. Pastoral counseling. 2. Crisis intervention (Mental health services) 3. Pastoral care. 4. Crisis management--Religious aspects--Christianity. I. Title.

BV4012.2.K38 2005
253.5--dc22

                                                                    2005048992

Printed in the United States
05 06 07 08 09 | 5 4 3 2 1

Author Photo: D.N. Premnath

Production Staff: Nelson Estarija, Robin Witkin, Susan Carter

Dedicated to my Steinbacher nephews and nieces — Bill (IV), John, Jim, Sue (Hammond), Linda, Karen, Cindy, Darrell (Hammond), and great-nephews and -nieces: Billy (V), Jaclyn, Sarah, Katie, Caitlin, Jimmy, Michael, Courtney (Ferrari), Cassie (Boisvert) and Marc (Hammond), who are living through the crises of the sudden and untimely deaths of
both
parents/grandparents

and

in memory of my brother William Henry Steinbacher III (1942–2004)

and

my sister-in-law, Anne Louise Scanlon Steinbacher (1943–2003),

who both died during the writing of this book.

Their lives — and deaths — are a testament to getting through crises with grace and courage.

Contents

Part 1: Background

Part 2: Cases

Preface

In the preface of my last book (*Complicated Losses, Difficult Deaths*, Resource Publications, Inc., 2000), I wrote that it was the hardest book I had written (vii). At that time I was experiencing the splitting of my parish into two separate communities and the multiple losses that split involved. Little did I know that five years later I would be writing a book on crisis care and I would be experiencing multiple *personal* crisis events, including the sudden deaths of my brother and sister-in-law, which would prompt me to once again say that *this* book is the hardest one I have written.

I write my books out of my personal and professional experience. I have been blessed with a temperament and with training that help me remain calm during crisis events and losses. Unfortunately, I have had a lot of practice. My brother, Bill, was the first to recognize my gift for dealing with crisis, and before he died I told him I was dedicating this book to him, and in memory of his wife who had died in December. I did not know at that time that I would be dedicating this book *in memory* of them both, as he would also die before the book was actually published.

It is my hope that this book will help fill what I see as a void in the field of crisis ministry resources. There are numerous good secular texts on crisis counseling, but many of the pastoral crisis texts are now outdated. This book is written for pastoral caregivers and ministry students who are trying to better understand and minister in crisis situations. It is written as both a theoretical and a practical guide for crisis ministers and reflects almost two decades of teaching and counseling experience.

Given my history I think that my next book will be about birthing or laughter or dancing or joy. It's worth a try.

Acknowledgments

This book draws on almost two decades of teaching and counseling experience and five decades of life experience. In particular I would like to acknowledge a few people who have been pivotal in the writing of this book:

— my Steinbacher family, to whom this book is dedicated

— my husband, Prem, and my children, Deepa and Micah, who continue to be the foundations of my life

— my employer, St. Bernard's School of Theology and Ministry, who granted me a sabbatical to write this book

— my colleague Deacon Tom Driscoll, who helped me with resources, encouragement, and suggestions for chapter 5

— my students and clients who have helped me to be a better teacher and counselor, particularly the students in my fall 2004 crisis class who read and responded to the rough draft of this text: Duane Beck, Virginia Clark, Tracy Morrall, Frank Pettrone, Mark Robbins, Paul Virgilio, and Judy Ward

— the staff at Resource Publications, Inc., who once again believed in the importance of my work; and in particular my new editor, Helen Nicole St.Paul, my sister on the journey

Part 1

Background

1

What Is a Crisis?

Definitions

Over the years the word *crisis* has become part of our everyday vocabulary. We often hear — or find ourselves saying — I'm having a crisis; he must be going through a midlife crisis; she's having a crisis of faith. We use the word as if it is some *thing* that happens *to* us, over which we have no control, an unwanted enemy. This is one *part* of the definition of crisis, but there is much more to this word that warrants our attention as pastoral ministers who are continually called upon to respond to people and communities[1] in crisis. Understanding crisis and knowing how to better respond to those experiencing crises are pivotal to ministering in today's world and church.

The word *crisis* comes from the Greek word *krinein* meaning "to decide." It is defined as a crucial time, a climax, or a juncture and is often depicted by the Chinese symbol that means danger *and* opportunity. Too often we have thought of and ministered to someone in crisis as if crisis is *primarily,* if not exclusively a *danger,* overlooking the *opportunity* for *growth.* It is important for us to know more about this complex word.

The most basic definition of crisis is that it is *an internal reaction to an external event* (Stone 19). This reaction may be experienced by an individual, a family, or a community; early crisis-intervention literature focused almost exclusively on the individual. The external event may be called a *crisis event,* although the event itself is *not* what defines a crisis. This is the first and most frequent mistake we make in talking about crisis; we define an *event* as a crisis, rather than our *reaction* to the event as the crisis. The *same* event that happens to *different* people will be experienced by some as crisis and by others as non-crisis. We experience an event, internally assess the event, and call upon our internal resources and coping mechanisms to respond to the event (ibid.). Only when these usual ways of dealing with things do *not* work does a crisis reaction develop. *It would be helpful, then, to distinguish between a crisis event and a crisis reaction and to understand that the two are not the same.*

Types of Crises

There are various types of crises, and it is important to know the range of definitions.

1. When most of us use the word *crisis,* we are referring to what is called a *situational* crisis; that is, our response to unpredictable, accidental, and unanticipated life events. This type of crisis event and reaction has also been referred to as *coincidental* or *accidental.* Examples of this type of crisis are a person's crisis reaction to the sudden death of a loved one, or a community's crisis reaction to the sudden removal of their pastor. It is this type of crisis event and reaction that is the focus of crisis intervention theory and that we commonly face as pastoral ministers. Andrew Lester further delineates situational crises into *interruptive*—having an external origin (personal, congregational, and public)—and *eruptive*—coming from within and often associated with strong feelings.[2] Much more will be said about this type of crisis and how we can better minister to those experiencing situational crisis reactions.

2. *Developmental* crises refer to our reactions to predictable life events or life passages, such as from teen to young adult, or from midlife to old age. We *all* experience these *life passages;* we do *not* all have a crisis reaction to them, yet the term for these life events remains *developmental crisis.* No wonder there is so much confusion and misuse of the word *crisis!* Developmental crises also refer to life passages that occur for many, but not everyone: such as from student to paid worker, from paid worker to student, and from paid worker to retired person. Again, only *some* people will experience these developmental changes as *crises.* These are the types of events and reactions that are referred to in statements such as, "He's having a midlife crisis." In regard to a community, a developmental crisis may occur as a community transitions from being a first-generation community of immigrants to a second- or third-generation multicultural community; or a developmental crisis may occur as a community transitions from being a new or young community to an established or aging community. Although these passages and reactions warrant our attention as pastoral ministers, most of us are

not qualified to counsel those experiencing developmental crises. We need to be able to assess a developmental crisis reaction and refer a person or community to professional help. *Standard crisis intervention models and skills are not designed for ministering to a person, family, or community experiencing a developmental crisis.*

Much of the literature on crisis intervention has focused on situational and developmental crises. More recent literature has added to the list of crises.

3. *Sociocultural* crises (Hoff, *People* 38) are situational crises that arise primarily from cultural values and social structures, and an awareness of these values and structures is crucial to understanding and ministering to the person, family, or community experiencing them. An example of a situational crisis reaction that is sociocultural for an individual is a job loss that occurs as the result of discrimination based on age, gender, race, disability, or sexual identity; for a community, it may be a parish's reaction to hiring a female pastor or pastoral administrator (gender issue). The pastoral minister needs to be aware of this added dimension to the crisis event—both to better minister to the individual, family, or community experiencing the discrimination, and to be a prophetic voice to address the societal factors that contribute to unjust discrimination.

4. An *existential crisis* reaction (James and Gilliland 6) is an inner conflict or anxiety that is experienced in reaction to an intrapsychic loss of a dream. An example of this is a woman who experiences an existential crisis reaction as she realizes that, childless at forty-six, she will never biologically conceive. The crisis event often remains unnamed by the person until she experiences an *acute crisis reaction* that has been developing over a number of years. This type of crisis reaction may *appear* to be *situational*. The childless woman seeks your counsel wondering why she feels so distraught upon hearing that her forty-two-year-old sister is pregnant with twins after twenty years of infertility. It is important for the pastoral minister to be aware that this is *more* than a situational crisis for the woman; her crisis reaction stems from her unfulfilled life's dreams, perhaps never openly expressed, to be a mother. For a community, this may mean realizing that their dream to be a thriving parish staffed with numerous priests may never be a reality.

5. *Environmental crises* are the results of natural or human-created disasters. Environmental crisis events include hurricanes, floods, earthquakes, forest fires, and blizzards (natural phenomena), as well as epidemics (biological), ethnic cleansing in war (political), or depression (economic) (ibid.). These crises usually affect entire communities — in the broadest sense — and require awareness of and training in communal models of crisis intervention.

6. A *transcrisis state* is a more recent term in crisis literature (ibid. 6–8). The duration of a situational crisis reaction is limited and the crisis reaction diminishes and is resolved within a short period (weeks). However, in some instances the original crisis event and reaction are not resolved but are *submerged*. The person believes the crisis is resolved only to have the crisis reaction *re-emerge* with the addition of new stressors in his life. Under new stressors the crisis reaction often becomes displaced toward someone else, such as the pastoral minister who may be confused by the sudden anger that comes her way. It is helpful for the pastoral minister to be aware that anger toward her may not be the result of a current crisis but may be the result of an *unresolved crisis* that is re-emerging. The original unresolved crisis reaction often occurs because of substance abuse, psychosis, personality characteristics, or ongoing environmental stressors (ibid. 7). Being able to identify a crisis reaction as a *transcrisis state* will allow the pastoral minister to refer the individual to someone specifically trained in working with transcrises, or to bring in a consultant to help the congregation work through their transcrisis state.

7. One final type of crisis reaction needs to be mentioned, PTSD, or post-traumatic stress disorder. Although this condition goes beyond the usual purview of crisis and beyond the usual capabilities of the pastoral minister, the minister must be aware of its existence and be able to recognize it. PTSD is an anxiety disorder that is caused by a severe trauma. A trauma is an event that is perceived as an acute or overwhelming threat. The core experience is one of disempowerment and disconnection; the core feelings are helplessness and intense fear. The person, family, or community experiencing PTSD feels a loss of control, a sense of isolation, or a threat of annihilation (Hermann 33–35). The original crisis event is a trauma. The pastoral minister needs to be able to identify the original crisis event as a trauma and to assess that the person, family, or community may be experiencing PTSD as a result of this event.

Referral and additional consultation or help will be crucial. The person or community experiencing PTSD may also be in a transcrisis state, but not everyone in transcrisis has PTSD (James and Gilliland 7).

EVENT → REACTION

Situational Crises *— MOST COMMON FOR MINISTERS TO RESPOND TO*

This book will focus specifically on *situational crises* as the most common ones that require a pastoral minister to respond. In order to more fully understand these crises, some more definitions are in order. A situational crisis is preceded by a crisis *event* that triggers a crisis *reaction.* Whereas the *same* event — the pastor leaving — does not trigger a crisis reaction in everyone, some events by their very nature are more *likely* to trigger crisis reactions in almost everyone — for example, the sudden death of a spouse or child, a diagnosis of terminal illness, or a terrorist attack.

Pastoral ministers need to be aware of events that will *likely* trigger crisis reactions in their parishioners. These events are of two types: hazardous events and precipitating events. The *hazardous event* is the *original* shock or event that triggers a crisis reaction — such as being fired from a job. The *precipitating event* is the *last-straw* event, the event that brings a parishioner to our door or propels a community into crisis. This event may be a minor event seemingly unrelated to the original, hazardous event, and we may be perplexed at the person's or the community's *seemingly* exaggerated reaction. The pastoral minister needs to be aware that the seemingly innocuous precipitating event may be the *last straw* in a series of events that are all linked to an original, hazardous event. Identifying the hazardous event is pivotal in crisis counseling. More will be said about this in chapters 2 and 3. *In many cases the hazardous and precipitating events are the same event.*

The pastoral minister should also be able to identify *situational crisis behavior,* such as tiredness, helplessness, confusion, anxiety, disorganization, immobilization, and physical symptoms (Stone 22). These behaviors may appear to be similar to depression, which is why the pastoral minister needs to be aware of other factors (such as a hazardous event) that will affirm a crisis diagnosis.

Crisis events are often *loss events* and a person or community in crisis may also be in the first phase of grief: shock and disbelief.[3] An

GRIEF

important difference here is that a person or community is in crisis for only a brief period—hours, days, or weeks—whereas grieving goes on for months and years. It may be helpful to think of ministering to people in crisis as *similar* to ministering to people in the first phase of grieving. Once the initial phase of crisis is over, we can continue our ministry by giving a referral for supportive grief counseling, or by having someone conduct grief counseling with our congregation.

Situational crises are time limited. Because our reaction is one of immobilization and confusion, we cannot stay in crisis forever. Not only is it too painful, but also we can't go on not going to work, not making decisions, or not knowing which way to turn. People in crisis are very vulnerable and very open to help. If we know how to respond and help, they will get through their crisis, function, and feel better. The temptation the pastoral minister must avoid is giving too much help. A drowning person needs a life preserver, or a rope, or strong arms to pull her up. Once she has help and is in no immediate danger, she can begin to help herself. She may need some reassurance (crisis care), but when she is okay (through the crisis), we can step away. Pastoral ministers often make the mistake of continuing to help too much after the crisis is over, or of not knowing which helping device to use, and therefore using none. In the twelfth century, Hugh of St. Victor wrote of three types of persons: those who have a flood within and no ark; those who have a flood within and an ark, but they are not *in* the ark; those who have a flood within, and an ark, and are able to get in and stay in the ark (Oden 4). Today, in the twenty-first century, this is an apt description of what it feels like to experience and survive a crisis event and reaction.

Some authors will go so far as to say that all (situational) crises are *religious* at their core because they involve ultimate issues such as suffering, life, death, and pain (Stone 16). It is a time when people may ask about the meaning of life. Why did God do this to me? (ibid. 28–30). This makes the pastoral minister the *best* person to respond to people in crisis, as she represents God's love, hope, grace, and faith in the midst of despair (ibid. 16).

History of Crisis Theory

To talk about crisis intervention is essentially to talk about a twentieth-century phenomenon, although people have experienced and been helped in crisis since the beginning of humankind. Scripture is replete with people and communities in crisis—such as Eve, Abraham, Hagar, Noah, Mary, Peter, Paul, the Israelites, and the early church—and what they did to survive.

The modern-day history of crisis intervention usually begins with Sigmund Freud's psychoanalytical theory. From Freud we gain the insight and knowledge that crisis can be helped through looking at a person's past emotional experiences. Freud determined that it was early-childhood fixation that caused an event to become a crisis (James and Gilliland 10). Freud also stated that his three-part model of the personality—id, ego, and superego—needs to be in balance, in a state of equilibrium, to avoid unhealthy defense mechanisms from forming (Hoff, *People* 8). Psychoanalysis is long-term and looks at a person's early childhood; modern crisis intervention is short-term and present-oriented. However, crisis intervention, and all counseling, owes Freud a debt for his pioneering work and for the concepts and insights that are still drawn upon in what is referred to as *expanded crisis theory* (James and Gilliland 10). Freud's concept of *catharsis*, expressing feelings about a trauma or crisis, is still pivotal to expanded crisis counseling today (Hoff, *People* 9).

Erich Fromm, Abraham Maslow, and Erik Erikson, known as ego psychologists, are often referred to as the next stage in crisis theory development. They developed less deterministic theories of human development that stressed the person's capacity to learn and grow throughout life. They have been attributed with providing the philosophical foundation for crisis theory (ibid.). The ego psychologists also shifted their research and counseling from the severely disturbed individuals who were the basis of Freud's work to more *normal* individuals.

In the mid-twentieth century, psychiatrists treating World War II and Korean War soldiers gave us additional insights and language for expanded crisis theory and intervention. Distressed soldiers were treated at the front lines and recovered sufficiently to be sent back to duty. This indicated that swift and immediate intervention was effective. Although today we may question whether the goal of crisis intervention is to send soldiers back to war, we glean our insights from what *was* done, not what we think *should* have been done.

Contemporary crisis theory often starts with the work of Erich Lindemann, as does contemporary grief counseling theory. In 1942 a fire destroyed the Cocoanut Grove Melody Lounge in Boston, killing 492 people. Lindemann did a study of the survivors of this disaster tracing their grief reactions. Because loss is linked with crisis, this study is a foundational document in contemporary crisis theory (Hoff 9). In 1964 Gerard Caplan wrote *Principles of Preventive Psychiatry,* focusing on preventing crisis through attention to social, cultural, and material factors. Subsequent theorists still quote and build upon Caplan's foundational public-health approach to crisis resolution. In the 1960s the community health movement emerged and emergency mental health programs were developed, and in the 1960s and 1970s the suicide-prevention movement came into being. This history has largely been a history of psychiatric theory. More recently attention has been paid to the social factors of crisis (Hansell; Hoff, *People*), and to cross-cultural and feminist influences in the field (Mawby and Walklate; Hoff, *Battered Women*). Expanded crisis theory today incorporates psychoanalytic, systems, adaptational, interpersonal, chaos, and ecosystem theory (James and Gilliland 10–14) and takes into account the systems and cultures within which we live.

As we can see, expanded crisis theory has had a largely psychological history, more recently acknowledging social and cultural factors and influences. Most histories and most crisis intervention texts still do not explore theological factors and influences. Whereas this text will not go into a detailed, expanded history by adding the theological factors, note that they are missing. This book is written for the pastoral minister, not for the psychologist or psychiatrist, because this author believes the pastoral minister is in the best position to provide effective crisis caring. More will be said about this in chapter 2.

2

The Unique Role of the Pastoral Minister As Crisis Caregiver

Poor immigrant woman is pregnant with child. Married boss is named father. Man reconciles with infertile wife by giving her free reign to punish woman. Pregnant woman flees from angry wife.

Unwed pregnant teen proclaims her virginity; fiancé supports her claim that she has had no sexual relations. They both claim it is a miracle from God. Family and friends are unsure.

These vignettes may sound as though they are torn from today's tabloids, but they are actually taken from the book of Genesis, chapter 16, and the Gospels of Matthew and Luke, chapter 1. The first vignette concerns Abram's wife, Sarai, who is unable to conceive, so Abram impregnates Sarai's servant Hagar (with Sarai's blessing). After Hagar conceives, she looks at Sarai "with contempt" (Genesis 16:5). Sarai complains and Abram tells Sarai to deal with Hagar as she sees fit. Sarai "dealt harshly with her" (6), and Hagar flees. The second vignette describes Mary of Nazareth, who is engaged to marry Joseph the carpenter; an angel tells her that she will conceive a child by the power of the Holy Spirit.

Scripture is filled with examples of people in crisis; Hagar and Mary are but two examples of this. Week after week, congregations hear stories from Scripture replete with people in crisis and how they respond to crisis events. Rarely, however, do ministers *preach* on the texts as examples of *people in crisis*. We will return to examples of this later in this chapter. *It is my contention that pastoral ministers are in a unique position to be crisis caregivers in all aspects of their ministries and need to claim and act on that privilege more frequently.*

Crisis Ministry As Pastoral Care

1. Crisis caring/ministry is part of the broader concept of pastoral care that is the responsibility of all members of communities of faith, under the leadership of recognized pastoral ministers.

In order to understand what it means to do crisis ministry, it is necessary to understand the broader context of pastoral care out of which it comes. The term *pastoral care* comes from the Latin term *cura animarum,* meaning "the cure or care of souls." A classic work from 1964 that traces the history of pastoral care throughout the history of the Christian church is *Pastoral Care in Historical Perspective* by William Clebsch and Charles Jaekle. They state, "The ministry of the cure of souls, or pastoral care, consists of helping acts done by representative Christian persons directed toward the *healing, sustaining, guiding,* and *reconciling troubled persons* whose troubles arise *in the context of ultimate meanings and concerns"* (4).[1] Clebsch and Jaekle divide the history[2] of the Christian church into eight epochs, noting that one *function* of pastoral care (healing, sustaining, guiding, or reconciling) was prominent in each epoch. For instance, in the early church, from the time of Christ to 180 CE, the emphasis was on *sustaining* souls in this world, while waiting for and anticipating an imminent end to the world; whereas during the Renaissance and Reformation, the emphasis was on *reconciling* individual persons to a righteous God. In the 1980s Howard Clinebell (43) has added the function of *nurturing* to the definition of pastoral care, and Edward Wimberly (19–21) has added the function of *liberating,* particularly in the African-American churches. The emphasis in these definitions is on *what* pastoral care *is,* and what *acts* comprise the care of souls in the church.

Wedded to the emphasis on the *functions* of pastoral care, however, is an equal emphasis on *who* can provide this care. Note in the definition from Clebsch and Jaekle, the emphasis is on *"representative Christian persons."* This definition, while sounding broad, in actuality became narrowed to ordained ministers and priests. Pastoral care, historically, was viewed as something the *ordained* leaders of the church *did.* The ordained leaders of the church were the caregivers and the parishioners were the care receivers. This definition has limitations for many reasons. First of all this definition, by emphasizing the history of the *Christian church,* ignores the *Judeo*-Christian heritage of pastoral care. The idea of caring for the members of one's religious community is not unique to Christianity. Don Browning argues that we cannot understand Christian pastoral care unless we understand its Jewish foundation. According to Browning, pastoral care in the early Christian church drew heavily upon the Jewish symbols of covenant and promise, combined with a Christian expectation of the coming kingdom (53–54). Jesus as *Jewish* prophet, wise man, and moral teacher influenced early Christian religious leaders, the first Christian pastoral caregivers.

A second limitation of the traditional definition is that *"representative Christian persons"* became restricted to *ordained* Christian persons, which in the Roman Catholic tradition became even further restricted to ordained, *celibate men.* This emphasis reflected the ecclesiology of the church until the Second Vatican Council, when the concept of the church as the *People of God* re-emerged. Thus we see a dramatic shift both in the leadership of the church throughout the last four decades, as well as in the definition of *who* provides pastoral care. Pastoral care shifts from being the domain and sole responsibility of the ordained leader of the community of faith[3] to being the domain and *responsibility* of *each member* of the worshiping community. In pastoral care literature definitions emerged, such as pastoral care is a ministry of the entire caring community, clergy *and* laity (Patton 3). In the churches this shift was reflected in the formation of pastoral care teams of lay members who visited the sick, consoled the bereaved, and cared for those in need.

John Patton describes this shift as a shift in pastoral care models from a *classical* and *clinical* pastoral model that emphasized the *message* and *care giver,* respectively, to a *communal contextual* model that incorporates the first two, but shifts the emphasis to the community of faith as those responsible for providing pastoral care (ibid. 3–5). Patton writes primarily from a Protestant perspective, but the shift also applies to the Roman Catholic Church. Roman Catholic Churches have also broadened definitions of ministry and pastoral care and who can provide this care. The emergence of lay ecclesial ministers and pastoral care teams are reflective of that shift. Pastoral care, today, may be defined as lifelong care that we give each other, grounded in our communities of faith (Karaban, *Isaiah* 3).

A final limitation of the definition of pastoral care must be mentioned, and this limitation is a new one. Whereas the traditional definition of pastoral care emphasizing *functions* is still appropriate today, the term *pastoral care* has also become intertwined with the term *pastoral counseling,* which has added a new restriction and limitation. The intertwining of pastoral care and pastoral counseling has resulted in an emphasis on training and professionalism, thus again restricting *who* can provide the caring or counseling. The definition of pastoral care has shifted to emphasize a counseling component of caring, while ignoring the history and broadness of the other functions of care, such as reconciling. We need to remember that pastoral care is the *broad* term that encompasses various *functions*—such as healing, sustaining, guiding, reconciling, nurturing, and liberating—and various *actions*— such as visitation, counseling, and spiritual guidance. We need also remember that pastoral care and counseling have become associated primarily with *diakonia* (service), but may also be associated with *kerygma* (proclamation), *didache* (teaching), and *koinonia* (community relationship with God) (Clinebell 66). Pastoral care is care provided by means of these functions and actions *throughout* a person's life; pastoral counseling occurs during *particular,* painful *moments* (Karaban, *Pastoral* 3). The pastoral counselor needs to emphasize advanced training in her work. The pastoral caregiver needs training to do various activities, but does not need to hold advanced degrees to be a caregiver.

Crisis ministry or caring falls in between pastoral care and pastoral counseling. In this book I am placing it within the realm of pastoral care and calling it *crisis caring* or *crisis ministry,* rather than crisis *counseling,* to emphasize that we are *all* called to do crisis caring for each other. Our pastoral leaders will be more equipped to do this, but we are *all* responsible for each other's care. I also place crisis caring within the context of pastoral *care* to broaden the concept of crisis caring *beyond* one-on-one counseling and to emphasize the *community* as the locus of care.

Crisis Ministry of the Whole Community

2. Crisis caring involves the care of the whole community of faith, not just individual members.

Because of the tendency to equate pastoral care with pastoral counseling, and because both pastoral care and pastoral counseling emphasized an individual, one-on-one relationship for so many years, crisis caring has tended to focus on an individual helper (carer) ministering to another individual in need (crisis). Charles Gerkin wisely reminds us that our emphasis on individual care is grounded in the Wisdom tradition with its focus on those who gave moral guidance to individuals; Browning said much the same. Gerkin argues for a retrieval of a broader foundation in both the Wisdom tradition *and* the priestly *and* prophetic traditions. The retrieval of the priestly tradition would place new emphasis on worship, and the retrieval of the prophetic tradition would place new emphasis on confronting issues of justice and morality (Gerkin 25).

SHIFT FROM SELF → COMMUNITY (BOTH)

The recent emphasis on the individual was largely influenced by events such as the privatism of the nineteenth century with its accompanying emphasis on a balanced, harmonious self (ibid. 49) and the influence of the development of psychology (twentieth century) with the accompanying emphasis on the self (ibid. 50). In more recent times, pastoral care and counseling have been influenced by a shifting ecclesiology with an emphasis on the community, as well as a shift in the field of psychology with an emphasis on systems thinking. The result for pastoral care and counseling, and thus crisis care and counseling, is a resurgence of caring for individuals, families, *and communities* in crisis. This need has been poignantly and tragically re-enforced by such recent events as school shootings, clergy sexual abuse, and the 9/11 terrorist attacks.

The Unique Role of the Crisis Minister

3. Although it is the responsibility of each member of a community of faith to provide pastoral care to other members, some members will desire to do this on a more formal and regular basis. It is these members who provide leadership in the various functions and actions of pastoral care. These members may be rabbis, ordained pastors, or lay ecclesial (pastoral) ministers. Part of their ministry will involve crisis caring.

Pastoral ministers—lay and ordained—have a unique role in crisis caring by virtue of their symbolic role and the nature of crisis. The symbolic role of the pastoral minister signifies that she represents something *more than* herself—a particular denomination, religious authority, or even God. A student once asked if I thought that in my role as pastoral counselor I was representing God. I found myself hesitating to say yes because it sounded haughty. Today I would have no hesitancy in saying yes. When I act in a pastoral leadership role, I may indeed be seen as representing God: God's love, forgiveness, acceptance, and mercy, along with God's judgment. Since crisis caring and counseling very often deal with threats to ultimate meaning — death, destruction, war, and terrorism — the pastoral minister is forced to contend with themes of transcendence, transformation, finitude, hopefulness, and resurrection. It is when experiencing a crisis that people are most likely to question the presence and nature of God in their lives. It is up to the pastoral minister to be the one ready and able to respond to these questions.

When people in crisis ask *why* questions in relation to God, they often ask the questions in three phases. The first time they ask, Why did God do this to me? they probably do not want or expect an answer; they simply want to be allowed to ask the question, which arises from their pain and anger. The second time they ask, Why did God do this to me? they are probably asking out of fear of being abandoned by God. The third time they ask, the question has probably become, Why does an all-good God allow suffering in the world? This is an example of what we call a *theodicy* question, and people who have experienced a crisis will expect their pastoral minister to be willing to engage in a theological discussion, offer workshops on this question, and preach about the nature of God. The pastoral minister may be wise to remind the person in crisis that we cannot always answer why, but that it is our belief as Christians that the *where* and *who* questions are just as important. *Where* is God in my suffering? *Who* is this God? The answer to these questions can be found in Scripture, tradition, and personal experience. Our God is a God who suffers and rejoices with us, by our side. Our God is a God who loves us enough to give us the Son, Jesus Christ, God-incarnate to remind and ensure us of God's love.[4] It is in our symbolic role as pastoral minister that we not only represent God and communities of faith, but that we minister through the traditions and rites of our faith — through prayer, worship, sacrament, and relationship (presence).

Crisis Ministry As Theological Affirmations

4. Pastoral ministers deal primarily with situational crises of understanding and decision (Allen 21–22). In response to crises of understanding, we need to emphasize remembrance, presence, and promise (Jeter 28) through our teaching, preaching, worship, rites, prayers, care, and counseling.

In times of crises of understanding, communities of faith desire a word from God — through God's representative, the pastoral minister — for their anger, confusion, guilt, and fear (Jeter 20). According to Joseph Jeter, when a pastoral minister responds to a crisis of understanding (theological crisis), she responds with *three* theological affirmations:

1. through remembrance, in worship, which is an act of remembrance

2. through presence, reminding our communities that God and we are with them in their pain

3. through promise, preaching and teaching that God is with us now and forever (ibid. 28–34)

As pastoral ministers we need to be prepared to respond to crises in our preaching, teaching, worship, caring, and counseling. This is done before, during, and in response to crisis. For communities of faith, a crisis may be personal, public, or congregational. If personal, it is a crisis of the pastoral minister himself; if congregational, it is something that affects the whole congregation; if public, it is something that affects the community inside and outside the congregation, such as wars, riots, and natural disasters (ibid. 13–14). Pastoral ministers need to be prepared to address these different types of crisis in *worship* by using familiar symbols, including prayers of lament, and by keeping the order of worship familiar, and thus comforting (ibid. 71–72). In *preaching* in the midst of crisis, pastoral ministers must remember to acknowledge and name the crisis, and then move to God's hopeful word for us (ibid. 105). Much more will be said about this in chapter 5.

The Unique Position of the Crisis Minister: Before and During Crisis

5. The pastoral minister is in a unique position to preach and teach about crises before they occur.

Pastoral ministers may set up Bible-study groups to study people and communities in Scripture who underwent crises. Pastoral ministers may also take the opportunity to preach on a biblical text from the standpoint of crisis, particularly when their community of faith is *not* in crisis. Using biblical texts involving Hagar and Mary, the Roman Catholic preacher would have the opportunity to preach on them at the following times: Hagar—Thursday of the Twelfth Week in Ordinary Time, year 1; Mary—Fourth Sunday of Advent and Christmas vigil.

6. The pastoral minister is in a unique position to do crisis caring—during a crisis.

As pastoral ministers we enjoy certain advantages that improve our ability to do crisis caring and counseling. We can respond with immediacy, we are available, and we have authority (Stone 14); we are approachable, trustworthy, and trained to deal with ultimate concerns; we do not have to keep to formal, fifty-minute hours; we can follow up and make home visits; we can reconnect our parishioners with God and communities of faith. We can take the initiative in a relationship, and we already have relationships with our community of faith; we have established rapport and trust as pastoral leaders. As *pastoral* ministers we are most attuned to and able to respond to the *spiritual* dimensions of crisis in our congregations.

As pastoral ministers we are also particularly equipped to help during four levels of crisis (Clinebell 184):

1. through pastoral care

2. through informal crisis counseling

3. through short-term formal crisis counseling

4. through longer-term, follow-up counseling (referral)

The Prophetic Dimension of Crisis Ministry

7. Being crisis carers connects us with the prophetic dimension of our ministry.

My favorite definition of pastoral counseling comes from Wayne Oates (*Pastoral*) and lays the foundation for understanding a prophetic dimension to crisis caring and counseling. Wayne Oates defines the pastoral counselor as the one who has a *prophetic* responsibility to go *beyond* the problems raised in the individual counseling relationship, and to address the *issues* raised in these relationships that point to pain, suffering, and oppression. A woman who is being sexually or physically abused comes to us in crisis. *One* responsibility we have is to address her pain and help her through her crisis and to safety. *Another* responsibility we have as *pastoral* crisis ministers is to address the systems of oppression, such as sexism, that contribute to, if not create, her being in crisis. Another person in crisis comes to us after being fired from his job because of racial prejudice or because he is openly homosexual. We need to address his pain in our care and counseling of him, but we also need to go beyond his individual pain to address racism and homophobia through our teaching and preaching.

Don Browning and Wayne Oates (*Pastoral*) were two of the first and only pastoral theologians to see clearly this component of pastoral counseling. Pastoral counseling and crisis counseling literature today still do not adequately or fully reflect the ethical and moral responsibility of the care we provide as pastoral leaders. My hunch is that we want to avoid the judgmental attitudes that pervaded much of our counseling and preaching for generations. In trying to correct this imbalance, however, we often now emphasize *only* God's love and acceptance without *also* addressing the morality and sinfulness of our actions. For instance, when a man comes to us and tells us he is having an affair, many pastoral counselors do a good job at exploring his pain and addressing the reasons for the affair. What we often fail to do is to give equal emphasis to addressing the morality and ethics of his actions. A maxim of pastoral counseling that I learned from Browning's writing is to address the pain *first*, while *temporarily bracketing* moral issues. Too often, however, the pastoral listener seems to forget to return to the moral issues.

The ideal time to address moral issues is, of course, *before and after* a person or congregation is in crisis. We do this through our teaching and preaching. This does not mean, however, that we *ignore* morality during a crisis. When Jesus spoke to the crowd surrounding the woman who was being stoned for committing adultery, he focused on the injustice of the actions of the crowd, "Let anyone among you who is without sin be the first to throw a stone at her" (John 8:7). Yet often when this passage is preached, we stress that Jesus is correcting the injustice of *only* the *woman* being punished for her action, thus addressing the sexism of the time. Or, there is an emphasis on Jesus *forgiving* (mercy) the woman for what she has done, pointing out that in the end the crowd did not condemn her for her actions and neither does he (John 8:10–11). What is often missed or underemphasized are his final words, "and from now on do not sin again" (John 8:11b). Jesus does not neglect ethics, morality, and sin—on an individual or a corporate level.

In this passage Jesus serves as the ultimate pastoral caregiver. He assesses and addresses the woman's immediate crisis; he goes beyond her situation and pain to address the system of injustice that causes her crisis (that only women be punished for an affair); and he returns to the ethics and morality of her actions by telling her to not sin again. Although it would be anachronistic to label Jesus as a crisis minister, we can see from this passage that he serves as the paradigm for us in *our* crisis ministry. In this passage he epitomizes all the qualities and attributes of crisis caregiver: personal, pastoral, and prophetic.

3

Individual and Communal Models and Theories of Crisis Ministry

A person, family, or community in crisis often evokes a kind of crisis reaction from the caregiver. Individuals, families, and communities in crisis display crisis behaviors and feelings, such as tiredness, helplessness, confusion, anxiety, and being paralyzed (Stone 21). They also experience altered cognition — that is, difficulty in sorting through events and feelings, difficulty in relating events, and inability to make decisions (Hoff, *People* 82). These feelings, behaviors, and cognitive responses *can* and often *do* evoke anxiety for the crisis minister. It can be difficult to sit with people in crisis. I have found it helpful to be familiar with a number of models of crisis intervention that can be easily remembered and referenced. I have also found it helpful to have a *non-anxious presence*. This chapter will detail various models of crisis intervention that can be used by the crisis minister. Chapter 4 will detail specific qualities, values, skills, and strategies that are important for crisis caring.

A number of years ago I received a phone call from a former student. She was at a friend's house many miles away. She described a very serious situation to me and asked what to do. Her friend's husband was in a barn at their house, with a gun, threatening to kill himself. She was upset, frightened, concerned, and anxious. She ended her description of the situation with, "I know I have taken a number of counseling courses with you, but right now I forget everything you ever taught me about crisis counseling." I was able to calm her down, remind her of some basic assessment and evaluation steps, and help her access her knowledge and skills so that she could appropriately and effectively intervene in the situation. (The man did not harm himself or anyone else.) I then followed up with her to see how everything went, including how she was doing.

Three Ways to Lessen Anxiety for the Crisis Minister

Not all crisis situations are this difficult for the crisis minister, but many are. It is essential that we as crisis ministers know how to handle our own anxiety as well as how to resource the models and tools we need to help others. Not all of us are comfortable being with someone in crisis. However, as pastoral ministers, we *will* be called upon to respond to people in crisis so we need to be able to manage our anxiety *enough* to respond. This will be discussed more fully in chapter 4. For now, I will mention this need and briefly describe three specific ways to lessen anxiety in the crisis minister.

1. *Imagery* — To reduce our anxiety level, we need to image the room with a finite amount of anxiety within it. As the person or people we are counseling grow more and more anxious, we can image them using up all the available anxiety so that there is little or none left over for us. As their level of anxiety increases, so will our level of calmness increase.

2. *Empathy* — We the caregivers are *not* the ones who have experienced a crisis event. It is not *our* job that is being cut, or *our* child who is ill, or *our* husband who is having an affair, or *our* family or community that is in crisis. We can emotionally distance ourselves from crises and reactions by using the skill of *empathy*—hearing and understanding the situation from the others' perspective. We do not *join with* them emotionally. We resist the temptation of putting ourselves in their place, or feeling sorry for their plight (sympathy).

3. *Knowledge of Skills and Models* — We also draw upon our knowledge of crisis skills and strategies (chapter 4) and models of intervention (this chapter) to appropriately and effectively minister to people in crisis.

A Variety of Individual Models and Strategies

A prerequisite for any crisis intervention is determining that a situational crisis exists. It is important to remember two things: (1) crisis intervention strategies, models, and skills are designed to work *only* in *situational* crises; and (2) crisis strategies, models, and interventions will work only if *a situational crisis exists.* Therefore, a prerequisite for looking at crisis models and interventions is the ability to understand how to *assess* whether a *situational crisis exists* (#2).

Assessment

A brief reminder of the definition of a situational crisis is helpful here. A situational crisis is our response to an unpredictable, unanticipated life event that evokes a crisis reaction, such as suddenly being fired from a job, experiencing the sudden death of a family member, or having a pastor suddenly removed from a community. The event (the firing, the death, or the removal) evokes a crisis reaction. We do not know what to do or how to cope. We feel immobilized by the situation and our reaction to it. We come for help in getting through the paralysis we feel in our crisis. We may not describe ourselves as being in crisis, but we will describe ourselves as not knowing what to do, or where to go, feeling lost, confused, and disoriented.

There are a number of ways we as pastoral ministers can determine whether people are in crisis:

1. *Observe behaviors and feelings to see if they can be classified as crisis behaviors.* Is the person, family, or community disoriented, confused, or at a loss as to what to do? Do they describe themselves as feeling immobilized or paralyzed? Are they anxious? Do they present themselves as helpless, vulnerable, and powerless?[1] Since these behaviors and feelings can also be indicative of grief, or even depression, we need to assess further to determine whether this is a crisis reaction.[2]

2. *Clearly identify a* **hazardous event** *that evoked the crisis reaction.* As we discussed in chapter 1, the *hazardous event* is the originating event that triggers the crisis reaction. Without an originating event, we are not looking at a crisis reaction. In order to find the hazardous event, we need to assess *what happened.* A person, family, or community in crisis may have difficulty determining *why* they feel as they do and *what* set them off. Or they *may* be able to tell us immediately of the event that evoked a reaction, such as getting fired, experiencing a death, or having the pastor removed. In either case, it is important to identify an *actual event* and *when* it happened. We do this by

asking *what happened* and *when* the person, family, or community *first* began to feel so upset. We help the person, family, or community put a time sequence to what feels like one overwhelming experience. Second, we work with the person, family, or community to see why this particular event has created such a distressing reaction for them (Hoff, *People* 75). If we cannot identify a hazardous event, the person, family, or community may not be experiencing a situational crisis.

3. *Look for a* **precipitating factor** – *that is, the* **last straw** *in a sequence of events that has brought the person, family, or community to our attention. A precipitating factor* may seem unrelated to a hazardous event. As the person, family, or community recount to us what seems like a rather minor event, we may wonder at their strong reaction to the event. Knowing that the person, family, or community may be relating only the *last* event in a series of experiences (the last straw), we can help them identify the *originating* event that began the reaction of crisis. Sometimes the precipitating factor and hazardous event are the same event, such as a sudden death, and that may make our assessment a bit easier. Knowing about and being able to identify precipitating factors will also help us assess whether the person, family, or community is in the *initial phase* of crisis, soon after the hazardous event; is in an *acute crisis state,* well into crisis behavior feelings and cognitions; or is experiencing *chronic stress* and reacting to stress, such as unemployment, over a long period. A reaction to chronic stress may be manifested in depression that has not been properly assessed and addressed and thus continues to be triggered with new stressors (ibid. 76). A helpful way to distinguish between initial, acute, and chronic crisis is to ask what brought the person for help *today* (ibid.).[3] This is particularly important if the distress seems to have existed for a long time.

4. *Look for what may be described as a feeling of* **cognitive dissonance.** Leon Festinger introduced the term *cognitive dissonance* in 1957. It is a phrase used to describe a feeling of distress that occurs when two sets of beliefs fail to align. When we are in crisis, perception and memory are altered. We cannot make decisions or solve problems, and may even have trouble in defining ourselves (ibid. 82). This inability is temporary, but jarring. Our usual perception of being organized, intelligent, and decisive, as an individual, a family, or a community, clashes with our present inability to respond. Our usual ability to think on our feet and respond with confidence seems to have disappeared. Being in crisis has evoked a dissonance of having

a certain set of beliefs about who we are, yet not being able to *do* any of the things we can usually do. This adds to our distress and confusion and anxiety.

5. *Look for a recent onset, a progression in distress, and a link to an event (Switzer).* David Switzer (*Minister* 41) suggests three questions that help us determine if a person is experiencing a situational crisis:

— Has there been a recent onset of the crisis feelings (anxiety, powerlessness, or vulnerability)?

— Have the feelings grown worse?

— Can the onset of the feelings be linked with an external (hazardous) event?

If the answer to all these questions is yes, it is yet another assessment indicator that we may be in crisis. Switzer has designed these questions for the individual in crisis; they may also be asked of the family or community in crisis.

6. *Continue our assessment of the crisis state on two levels.*

Level 1 — We must ensure the safety of the person in crisis and those surrounding him. We can do this by asking some key questions:

— Is there a threat to the life of the person in crisis or others?

— Is the person suicidal, homicidal, or violent? (Hoff, *People* 73).

Level 2 — This comprehensive crisis evaluation looks at the following questions:

— Can the person function in everyday life?

— What factors are related to their ability to cope and how can they be addressed?

— What is the hazardous event?

— Is the person in initial or acute crisis?

— How is the person coping or responding?

— What are their resources? (ibid. 74).

These questions can be used with families in crisis but are not as easily transferable to the community in crisis; however, some aspects of the questions may be used. In assessing the community in crisis, we may ask:

Level 1

— Is the community exhibiting destructive behavior toward themselves or others?

Level 2

— Is the community functioning in their day-to-day activities?

— How are they coping?

— What are their resources?

— Are they able to agree on a hazardous or precipitating event?

— Where are they in their crisis?[4]

Answers to these questions will help us describe a person's, family's, or community's *crisis plumage* (Hansell) — what distinguishes the person, family, or community in crisis from someone or some family or community that is *not* in crisis. Crisis plumage is a series of *distress signals* that people who are struggling with crisis send out. These signals range from difficulty with managing feelings and an inability to effectively resource help to suicidal or homicidal thoughts, substance abuse, and difficulty with the law (Hoff, *People* 78). For a community, this may be reflected in difficulty in expressing feelings, an inability to name the source of the difficulty, and self-directed and other-directed destructive behaviors such as undermining pastoral authority, discontent with the community, and blaming the pastor or others in authority.[5]

Because situational crises are reactions to *unexpected* life events, it would seem that we can't prepare for them and can only assess and respond *after* they happen — that is, secondary intervention. However, because certain events such as rape, sudden death, and natural disasters *tend* to evoke crisis reactions for many, we *can also* address situational crises *before* they occur — primary prevention. We can do this through identifying and ministering to individuals, families, and communities that are likely to be at risk. This can be done in our teaching, preaching, and counseling and will be addressed in chapter 5.

Models and Strategies: For Individuals[6]

Much of the literature on crisis care focuses on the *individual* in crisis. As pastoral ministers involved in crisis caring of individuals, these models are helpful.

ABC (Jones 87)

A basic model of intervention comes from Warren L. Jones, a psychiatrist. Many theorists refer to and have added to this model.

A. Achieve Contact — This is done *before* and *during* our time with the person in crisis. As pastoral ministers, we have *already* established relationships with those in our worshiping communities. It is partly *because* of this previous relationship that we may not have to spend much time connecting. However, we may not personally know the person who approaches us, and more work will need to be done here. This is a time to focus, attend, be nonjudgmental, and empathize.

B. Boil the Problem Down to Its Basics — This is the active phase of the intervention replete with direct, open, and closed questions. This is a time for gathering the essential data of the crisis. What happened? When? Where? How did it affect you? Who were you with? What happened next? This is not a place for a detailed history of a person's life. This is all about focusing.

C. Cope Actively — Formulate an action plan, short term and long term. Formulate alternatives. Help the person identify internal and external resources and connect them to these resources. Get the person to commit to action and to follow-up.

The specific strategies and skills for these models will be detailed in chapter 5.

ABCD (Clinebell 205–208)

A. Achieve a Trusting Relationship

B. Boil the Problem Down to What Is Important

C. Challenge the Person to Take Action on One Part of the Problem

D. Develop an Ongoing Plan for Action

Howard Clinebell is one of the theorists who have built on Jones's ABC model. Clinebell's model is essentially the same, with the addition of developing an action plan (that Jones implies in C).

Contact — Focus — Cope (Switzer)

1. Contact — Establish a relationship; identify presenting problem and precipitating factor.

2. Focus — Explore the situation and identify the threat.

3. Cope — Identify problem-solving resources; assist in making decisions; summarize new learning (Switzer, *Crisis* 132–161; *Minister* 65–89; *Pastoral* 49–52).

Switzer's model builds on Jones's ABC model and is similar to Slaikeu's model.

Components of Psychological First Aid: A Five-Step Model (Slaikeu 108–109)

1. Make Contact — Listen for facts and feelings; show empathy and concern.

2. Explore the Problem — Ask about the precipitating event, precrisis functioning (past), basic functioning, resources, lethality, and decisions.

3. Examine Solutions — Look at what has been tried, what more can be done, and alternatives.

4. Help in Taking Action — Contract for action collaboratively or directly.

5. Follow Up — Obtain identifying information; contract for reconnecting.

Slaikeu's model is clear and adequately delineates the steps of crisis counseling from a psychological perspective. It is harder to remember (no catchy acronym) and does not take into account an overtly ministerial perspective or theological language.

Six-Step Model (James and Gilliland 33–35)

1. Define Problem from Client's Perspective

2. Ensure Safety of Client

3. Provide Support

4. Look at Alternatives

5. Make Plans

6. Get Commitment

James and Gilliland assume a relationship and do not emphasize establishing contact. They spell out important additional steps that are described in Jones's and Clinebell's writing but are not overtly spelled out in the phrases (ABC or ABCD) that describe the model. The critique of Slaikeu holds here: More steps are helpful, but harder to remember; the model is geared toward the secular counselor.

Four-Stage Model (Hoff, *People* 28)

Each of the models presented thus far has its advantages and disadvantages. What could be easier than remembering ABC? Yet by remembering only the acronym, we may not remember all the details that go along with each stage. James and Gilliland's six-step model is the most comprehensive model and should certainly be referred to when studying crisis models. Personally, I have found Hoff's four-step model the most helpful because it is easy to remember and incorporates all the essentials of good crisis counseling:

1. Assess

2. Plan

3. Implement

4. Follow Up

As part of the assessment process, Hoff includes ensuring client safety and the safety of others (step 2 of James and Gilliland). What she calls intervention and planning incorporate the skills and strategies that will be covered in the next chapter. Follow-up is particularly important and compatible with crisis *ministry*. Though Hoff is *not* writing particularly for pastoral ministers, she does include clergy as those who *first* come into contact with those in crisis (Hoff, *People* [4th ed.] 6).

Newer Models

It will be helpful to mention two final models here: the *equilibrium model* and the *cognitive model* (James and Gilliland 13–17). The equilibrium model views people in crisis as in a state of psychological disequilibrium; the goal of crisis intervention for this model is getting a person back to precrisis equilibrium (Caplan, *Approach*). This model may be used most appropriately early on in the crisis (initial crisis). The cognitive model purports that crises have their origins in faulty *thinking* about the events or facts surrounding the (hazardous) event (Ellis). This model promotes recognizing and changing irrational thinking with rational thinking. This model aims at correcting negative messages and turning them into positive, affirming self-statements. This method seems to work best after a person has stabilized a bit.

I encourage the reader to pick the model that is most appealing and memorize it. I have also created my *own* model, combining elements of a number of models, maintaining a catchy acronym, and adding a ministerial dimension:

CARING (Karaban)

1. Connect — Center, attend, and be present physically, emotionally, and spiritually.

Skills: Presence

2. Assess

— Does a situational crisis exist?

— Is the person functioning in everyday life? Is the person a threat to self or others (lethality)?

— What is the main concern? How has the person dealt with problems in past? Why is that not working this time?

— What are the resources—physical, emotional, and spiritual?

Skills: Assessment, Empathy, Probes, and Information Questions

3. Respond — Initially respond through continued empathy and assessment; begin to summarize; order and prioritize what happened and where the person is in relation to the crisis.

Skills: Assessment, Empathy, Summary, and Leverage

4. Intervene — Continue responding by actively intervening in the crisis situation, by setting up concrete short- and long-term action plans, and by giving the person direct feedback and information on where he or she is and what the options are.

Skills: Information Sharing, Self-Disclosure, and Immediacy

5. Network — Call upon and contact resources necessary to help the person through the crisis.

Skills: Information Sharing and Referral

6. Get Together — Set a definite time to meet again and follow up with how the person is doing.

Skills: Information Sharing

This model will be discussed in more detail in chapters 6 through 9 when we analyze particular crisis cases.

Models and Strategies: For Family Systems and Communities

Family: ABCX / Roller-Coaster (Hill)

In 1949 Reuben Hill described the crisis reaction to war-induced separation and reunion in terms of family stress and presented a framework of how a crisis develops in a family:

1. The Stressor Event (A Factor)

2. The Family's Resources for Meeting the Crisis (B Factor)

3. The Family's Understanding of the Event © Factor)

4. The Family Crisis (X Factor)

Hill further delineates how the crisis is played out in the family. There is:

5. A Time of Disorganization

6. A Time of Recovery

7. A Time of Reorganization

Hill's model is very similar to the ABC model, but it takes into account that a whole family may be experiencing, and therefore defining and reacting to, a crisis situation. This model corrects for addressing a crisis only from one individual's perception or reaction. This model is especially helpful when the hazardous event clearly impacts the whole family unit, such as the death of a parent. The model, however, does not clearly delineate *how* to *respond* or *minister* to the family in crisis.

Double ABCX Model (McCubbin and Patterson)

McCubbin used Hill's ABCX model to develop the Double ABCX model of family behavior in response to serious illness:

1. a Stressor (A Factor)

2. aA Buildup of Stressors (aA Factor)

3. b Resistance Resources (B Factor)

4. bB Adaptive Resources (bB Factor)

5. c Perception of Stressor © Factor)

6. x Crisis (X Factor)

7. cC Understanding and Meaning (cC Factor)

8. Coping Strategies for Adaptation

McCubbin classifies Hill's model (ABCX) as precrisis family factors, adds postcrisis factors (aA, bB, cC, and coping strategies), and stresses family adaptation over time.

In 1990 Mullen and Hill wrote an article that explores how pastoral caregivers are at pivotal places for influencing particularly the bB Factor, the resources families acquire and use in coping with the crisis. They argue that pastoral caregivers are the embodiment of grace for families in crisis (253). Pastoral caregivers are also in critical positions to influence the cC Factor, the new meanings families develop to understand their crisis. Mullen and Hill point out that it is in redefining a crisis and giving it new meaning that families are best able to cope and adapt (255).

Expanded Crisis Theories (James and Gilliland)

James and Gilliland describe newer models that take into account the environmental, social, and situational factors not adequately addressed by earlier individual, psychoanalytically oriented theories as part of *expanded crisis theory* (10). They argue that newer, expanded crisis theories, and thus models, draw not only from psychoanalytical theory but also from systems theory, adaptational theory, interpersonal theory, and chaos theory (10–13). They argue that a whole new theory of crisis intervention called *ecosystem theory* is evolving (13). This theory takes into account not only a person or family's personal, social, and financial resources but also the total ecological system of a person (14). Whereas a detailed description of these theories is beyond the purview of this book, it is important to note their existence as an indicator of what is happening in the field of crisis theory and intervention. This especially impacts the pastoral minister who is providing crisis care for a whole congregation in crisis.

Psychosocial Model (James and Gilliland)

Finally, there is the *psychosocial model* that stresses the influence of the social environment. This model goes beyond defining crisis as an internal reaction to an external event that resides only in an individual. This model goes outside the person and addresses the systems that impact the person that need to be changed; proponents include Alfred Adler, Erik Erikson, and Salvador Minuchin. This is the model most compatible with crisis care in a community of faith. I agree with James and Gilliland, who take an eclectic approach. The many models and theories are mentioned to demonstrate the breadth and scope of the field.

CARING for Communities

For congregational crisis caring, I build on my basic CARING model by adding the following elements:

1. Connect — Additional elements for community caring: Importance of connecting to the community as a whole as well as individually.

Skills: Using teaching, preaching, worship, and prayer to establish and build a broader connection.

2. Assess — Additional elements: Importance of being aware that in a community crisis there are a variety of reactions: some will be in crisis; some will not. Importance of identifying and agreeing on what has triggered the crisis.

Skills: Enhanced assessment skills and knowledge of systems theory

3. Respond — Additional elements: Initial response will include a willingness to seek consultation with other professionals as the pastoral minister himself may be the cause of the crisis or may be caught up in a congregational crisis.

4. Intervene — Additional elements: Intervention will take place on a corporate level through teaching, preaching, prayer, and worship, as well as counseling.

5. Network — Additional elements: The minister herself will need the resources that are resourced.

6. Get Together — Additional elements: The congregation *and* the minister need to follow up.

4

Responding to Crises: Pastoral Qualities, Values, Skills, Principles, and Conditions

Crisis counseling skills and strategies work only *when a situational crisis exists.* Chapter 3 spent considerable time delineating ways to assess whether a crisis exists and describing various models that present an overview of how to approach the person, family, or community in crisis. This chapter is devoted to describing specific qualities, values, skills, and strategies that will enhance our ministry of caring for people in crisis.

Skills and strategies are helpful *tools* in doing crisis ministry. My particular approach to teaching pastoral care is a skills approach — teaching basic listening skills necessary for doing good pastoral care. However, these skills are always taught within the broader framework of different models of counseling, and those models are looked at within the broader context of what it means to be doing pastoral care. The skills that I will be referring to have their basis in the work of Gerard Egan, a Roman Catholic priest and professor of psychology. His book *The Skilled Helper* is now in its seventh edition and is used across the country in both secular and pastoral care and counseling courses. I am comfortable and familiar with his language, and because of its wide use, I believe it may be familiar to many of the readers of this book. Adaptations of the skills are mine and their application to crisis ministry is my own interpretation.

Before detailing the skills and principles of crisis care, however, it is important to look a bit more closely at the person providing that care — the pastoral minister. What are the *qualities* of an effective crisis caregiver?

Qualities and Values of the Crisis Minister

Many authors have lists of qualities or characteristics that are essential to the pastoral minister. Focusing on this assumes that the person and personality of the caregiver are important, a point that was assumed in the model of pastoral care referred to as *clinical pastoral.* This is the model that has held sway since the 1960s and was only recently replaced by what Patton refers to as the *communal contextual model* (4–5). It is the clinical pastoral model that emphasizes the personhood of the pastoral minister *and* the importance of the pastoral relationship. Although there has been a shift in the way we *do* care, I believe that there is still an emphasis on the person or people providing this care. Therefore, *a prerequisite for **doing** crisis ministry is having certain qualities that are foundational to **being** a crisis minister.*

More than fifty years ago Wayne Oates wrote a book called *The Christian Pastor.* Although now outdated, his is one of the first lists in the literature that refers to the importance of the qualities of the minister. His list is based on an interpretation of the later epistles; he states that pastors must be healthy and good teachers, willing workers, good managers of their own households, of sound mind, and above reproach. All of these qualities could be applicable today. He also states that pastors should *not* be new converts or divorced and remarried (72), characteristics that may be questioned in today's world. In 1989 David Switzer modified a list of qualities originally suggested by Mayeroff in 1971 that includes knowledge, an ability to be self-reflective, patience, trust, honesty, humility, hope, and courage (Switzer, *Pastoral* 15–16). John Patton extends the need for basic qualities to *all* members of communities of faith who do pastoral care and lists what he describes as *qualifications* for doing pastoral care: an understanding that who we are cannot be separated from what we do in ministry; a serious involvement in faith education, an awareness of how our relationship with our own family can impact the way we respond to families, an ability to handle personal issues objectively, a commitment to the importance of faith in our own lives, and a willingness to work (73–74). Gerard Egan focuses on the *relationship* and describes *values* that he sees as essential to the relationship. He lists respect, empathy, genuineness, and client-empowerment as foundational values in a helping relationship (46–58).[1] James and Gilliland list poise, creativity, flexibility, energy, quick mental reflexes, tenacity, ability to delay gratification, reality orientation, calmness under duress, optimism, positive self-concept, courage, objectivity, and faith in humanity's ability to overcome odds as essential traits (19–20). There are certainly more lists of qualities that can be mentioned. Those referred to here are ones that have influenced me and have contributed to the list that I have come up with. What follows is my list of what I refer to as *qualities* and *values* that I see as important in crisis ministers and crisis relationships:

Qualities

1. Respect — Respect is the most basic quality necessary for being a crisis minister. Respect implies a valuing of others simply because they are created in the image and likeness of God. It implies tolerance—honoring the person, family, or community because of who they are, not because of what they have or have not done. It is what Carl Rogers originally referred to as *unconditional positive regard* (283–284), a positive attitude toward others without regard to their actions. Respect is an attitude we also have toward ourselves and toward the world. It means taking care of ourselves physically, emotionally, and spiritually, as well as taking care of all of God's creation—people and the world in which they live. Respect also implies openness, an openness to hearing actions that may be distasteful and even abhorrent to us.

2. Caring and Compassion — It is my assumption that we are in ministry because we *care* about people. When others are in pain or in need of help, we are also pained and desire to help them with their pain. As God cares for us, we desire to care for others. Another word for this caring may be *compassion,* or what may be defined as an *awareness* of others' distress accompanied by a *desire to alleviate* it. Compassion is feeling pain *for* people who are in pain without getting drawn *into* their pain. It involves an *awareness* that pain exists, an *ability* to sense and feel others' pain, and a *desire to help heal* that pain.

3. Prudence — Being a crisis minister means being a person who has a down-to-earth attitude about life. Many of the problems (crises) brought to us will not take advanced-level knowledge or skills. There is a simplicity to crisis intervention models that is easy to grasp and appeals to a pragmatic personality. As crisis ministers we must resist our own curiosity and the temptation to go off on tangents. We must be able to keep the very real details of a situation in sight as we plan with those in crisis how to proceed. We must, in my opinion, be *prudent persons,* people who make *wise* and *sensible* choices that involve knowing *how* and *when* to act.

4. Courage — Being with people in crisis is not for the fainthearted. As crisis ministers we are asked to listen to difficult stories of death and destruction that may seem overwhelming. In helping people in crisis, such as battered women, we could also be putting ourselves in danger. It takes *courage* to listen to tales of trauma without giving in to despair. A synonym of courage is tenacity, or mettle, the strength to face danger or difficulty with fortitude. Crises present danger and opportunity. As crisis ministers we need courage to face difficulties and pain; we also need courage to help people in crisis stand up to and persevere through the difficulties of the crisis.

5. Genuineness — Being genuine complements being prudent. Another word for this is being *congruent* or, I would say, being human. As we listen to a sad or difficult story, we do not respond with neutrality but with what we are feeling inside—sadness, outrage, or compassion. We may temper our reactions as we counsel, but we do not deny we have feelings. We do not sit immobile as we hear of injustice and evil. We let people in crisis know that what they say affects us. We let our insides match our outsides. I tell my students, "I do not let my mouth drop to the floor. I practice prudence; but I do say wow a lot. I am genuine."

6. Assertiveness — Crisis counseling requires us to be listeners who are willing to participate in the process. It requires a willingness and an ability to be *assertive*—to ask questions, formulate plans, and take action. Crisis caring is *not* for those who prefer to listen without speaking. Crisis caring requires crisis ministers to have confidence in ourselves and in our abilities and a willingness to step forward. Those of us who believe it is impolite to interrupt or who prefer to let the other person speak may have trouble being a crisis minister. There is a certain *boldness* that is required of crisis ministers. We need to be able to insert ourselves into a conversation or even a situation.

7. Non-anxious Presence — This quality was referred to in the last chapter. To be present means to be *with* someone physically, emotionally, and spiritually. We convey this nonverbally with eye contact, touch, head nodding, and facial expressions. We also do this verbally. To be present in a non-anxious way means to be able to listen without getting caught up in the story. It means still having feelings but separating what is being said from ourselves enough to avoid being caught up in the storyteller's anxiety. To be present spiritually means being able to center ourselves, to call upon God's help, and to open ourselves to feeling God's presence within us. We can do this if we can remain calm, open, and receptive. We can listen non-anxiously if we truly understand the value and skill of *empathy*.

Values

1. Empathy — Empathy is both a value and a skill. I include it as my first value because I believe the crisis counselor must hold empathy in the highest esteem. Empathy is a willingness to understand the world from another person's perspective. It means putting our own agenda and story aside to hear what someone is going through from their point of view. To hold empathy as a value means that we truly honor the validity, perspectives, and experiences of others as much as our own and that we are willing to listen to those perspectives and experiences *first* so that we may be of help. Egan also lists empathy as a value and a skill. He notes that empathy as a value is a commitment to understanding clients from their unique points of view and the feelings surrounding their points of view; it is a commitment to understanding clients through the context of their lives; it is also a commitment to understand dissonance between a person's point of view and the reality of life (49).

2. Faith — Faith (belief and trust in God and God's goodness and power) is foundational for a crisis minister. The most basic definition of pastoral counseling is counseling that acknowledges that the healing that takes place in the counseling relationship is due not only to the skill of the counselor, the ability of the client(s), and the relationship between the client and counselor, but it must also be attributed to God's healing power at work within the minister and the person or people in need. Being a crisis counselor can be overwhelming and disheartening. We hear horrific stories of torture, abuse, death, and devastation. It is our belief (faith) in a loving God who companions us and suffers with us that sustains us and allows us to do our work.

3. Hope — Complementing faith is the value of hope—expecting and even *knowing* that balance, growth, and new life can and *will* be attained once more. People in crisis are often without hope. They do not see alternatives, possibilities, and open futures. They see only dead ends, despair, and closed doors. It is up to the crisis minister to see beyond the present, *seeming* hopelessness of a situation to a new and different future. This takes optimism, creativity, and, most of all, *hopefulness* on the part of the crisis minister. Because we have experienced growth and resurrection in crisis and have seen this happen in those to whom we minister, we can find and speak — in counseling, preaching, and teaching — of hope to those who have lost all hope.

4. Justice — To hold justice as a value means being committed to equality, fairness, and impartiality. It means honoring the rights of all humans to be treated equally and fairly. For crisis ministers this means we approach all people in crisis as deserving our care, before knowing the nature of the crisis (which they may have unjustly caused). It also means being committed to identifying and changing unjust systems that contribute to crisis, such as discrimination that contributes to unjust firing and sexism that contributes to unequal treatment of women. To hold justice as a value assumes that we as crisis ministers take seriously a prophetic dimension to our ministry.

5. Competency — Although we do not need doctoral degrees to practice crisis ministry, if we hold competency as a value, we should have a certain amount of knowledge and education in order to be competent and effective crisis ministers. The form this takes will differ from person to person. For some this may mean formal course work; for others it may mean supervised training programs. Everyone in crisis ministry should have a formal understanding of crisis intervention and experience in doing crisis care, preferably under supervision.

6. Morality and Ethics — Pastoral care and counseling, of which crisis ministry is a part, incorporates ethics and morality into its very foundation and fiber. As pastoral ministers we are committed to knowing the ethical standards of our field as well as the legal counterparts, such as reporting abuse and breaking confidentiality when someone is suicidal or homicidal. As crisis ministers we hold moral conduct as a value in our personal lives and in the work we do with those in crisis. As crisis *ministers* we also address ethics and morality with those to whom we minister, counsel, teach, and preach.

7. Multiculturalism — As crisis ministers in today's multicultural world, we hold the existence and benefit of a multicultural perspective as a value. We are aware that those to whom we minister are diverse and that we must be aware of our lack of knowledge, sensitivity, acceptance, or valuing of perspectives, ideas, customs, and cultures that differ from our own. Holding a multicultural perspective as a value means avoiding cultural stereotyping, identifying and owning our own biases and blind spots, taking diversity training, getting supervision on multicultural issues, and keeping the quality of respect and the value of justice paramount in our work.

Skills Necessary for Doing Crisis Ministry

Elsewhere[2] I have delineated the skills necessary to do good grief ministry. That list was based on my reinterpretation of the work of Gerard Egan. Here I will list the skills I believe are necessary for good crisis care, again building on Egan's work. Whereas the names and basic classification are Egan's, the explanations, additions, and adaptation to crisis work are mine.

1. Presence — Egan refers to presence as attending—that is, being with another physically and psychologically. I prefer to call this skill presence and to add being with a person physically, emotionally, and *spiritually*. I would also add that this presence needs to have a *non-anxious* quality. Presence, then, *first* happens *inside* crisis ministers. We are in touch with our own feelings and state of mind and our own openness to listen. We are able to quiet our inner self and to become calm. We do this through centering ourselves, asking God for help and guidance, and giving ourselves an internal pep talk, assuring ourselves that we have done this before. Once we are non-anxious and centered, we will be able to convey this to the person in crisis. Our calmness, confidence, and willingness to hear people in crisis will be conveyed through:

- our *physical attending posture*—eye contact, head nodding, and open posture

- our *emotional and psychological attending posture*—open, centered, calm, and confident

- our *spiritual attending posture*—connected to God's presence and healing power, spiritually grounded, and able to see God present in the person/people in crisis

41

This willingness and ability to be present is a prerequisite for doing any type of ministry, but particularly crisis ministry.

2. Assessment — Assessment is listed here as a separate skill (not in Egan) because it is so essential for crisis ministry. Assessment as a skill involves a knowledge of what constitutes a crisis, and an ability to call upon assessment questions: Has there been a recent onset of your feelings? Can you identify a particular event that provoked your thoughts, feelings, or behaviors? Are you able to function in your everyday life? Have you had thoughts of doing harm to yourself or others? Assessment makes use of another skill—information questions—with the goal being assessing whether a situational crisis exists and the level of distress related to the crisis.

3. Referral — After assessing whether a crisis exists, what type it is, and the level of distress and functioning (Hoff 82), we may decide that a referral is necessary. Referral can be hard under any circumstances, but it may be especially difficult when dealing with a person in crisis. In a noncrisis situation, we will refer to another helper or agency when the problem presented goes beyond our training and expertise, when we have a strong emotional response to the people (positive or negative), and when we believe that the problem calls for long-term therapy.[3] To do this, we must believe that referral is a good and necessary tool, know when it is necessary, know good referral sources,[4] and be able to make a referral with confidence. All these principles apply also to crisis counseling, but we do not always have the luxury to apply them. Suicidal people may be beyond our expertise and we may have a strong reaction to them, but if we try to refer without first intervening, they may act on their suicidal thoughts. Referral in these cases may mean calling in another resource to help us act in the person's best interest rather than sending him or her to another resource. In a less severe crisis, we may refer a person to another helping agency, but we may also go *with* the person to the agency or call and check that he or she has contacted the agency. How we do our referrals in crisis counseling depends not only on our own limitations but also on the severity of the crisis and the level of distress in the person. See the cases in part 2, chapters 6–9, for examples of doing referral in crisis situations.

4. Empathy — The skill of empathy is pivotal to any type of listening. Empathy is the ability to hear and understand, and to communicate understanding of the world from the perspective of the people in crisis. We are focused on the people speaking.

Although what they say may sound similar to something we have been through—divorce, death, or job loss—we are listening to their story through their perspective and to how an event has impacted them. We listen to the *content* of what is said as well as to the *feelings* behind the content. In grief counseling we convey our empathy with statements such as: If I have heard you correctly, what you are saying is _____.

Although the concept of empathy is pivotal to crisis counseling, we will not be *conveying* empathy in the same way. We will be using empathy as a *background* and *foundation* to all that we do, but we will *not* be conveying empathy through the usual empathic statements. Instead, we will primarily be using *information questions and information sharing* as our communication skills.

5. Information Questions — People in crisis are often overwhelmed by what is happening to them and within them. This means that the crisis minister needs to be active and assertive in helping persons in crisis to relate their story with some focus, clarity, and order. The best skill for doing this is what I call *information questions.*[5] These are questions such as:

— What happened? When?

— Where were you? Who were you with?

— Then, what happened?

— What did you say? How did they respond?

These are open questions. We may also need to get very specific and ask closed, yes or no questions, such as (in relation to being fired):

— Did he actually say you were fired?

— Were there any options or a time frame given?

— Are you able to go to work?

— Do you have any other job options?

Whether our questions are open or closed will depend on the ability of the person in crisis to speak. By asking questions we as crisis ministers are *quickly* gathering information to *assess* and *understand* the situation so that we may *respond* and help.

6. Information Sharing — Information sharing is information conveyed *by* the crisis minister *to* the people in crisis. This may be a sharing of resources, strategies, or a crisis plan. This requires an active role on the part of crisis ministers. After we have assessed and responded to the person in crisis, we offer possibilities, options, and resources. Whereas information sharing is usually done sparingly in other types of counseling, it is one of the *primary* skills used in crisis counseling. This skill requires crisis ministers to know resources and to be able to access them quickly and to summarize them to the person in crisis.

7. Summary (Summarizing) — Summary is a type of empathy, but it is done less frequently. It still requires that crisis ministers listen to the perspective of the person and understand that perspective. In crisis counseling, summary would be used periodically to check to see that the crisis minister is getting the story straight.

— Let me stop and summarize the situation as I have heard it thus far.

— Let me summarize the options we have gone over for you.

Being able to summarize well requires careful listening, being able to prioritize and order important facts and feelings, and being able to put what we heard in our own words. Part of this skill comes from being centered and focused (presence), and part of it comes from practice.

8. Leverage — The skill of leverage involves prioritizing issues and concerns. People often present a number of issues without a clear sense of what to work on first. Leverage helps a person to choose the *one* issue or problem that will affect all others. In crisis counseling, leverage means dealing with the crisis problem *first* by helping the person identify the crisis event and focusing on the crisis reaction. Leverage questions include:

— What is my *main* concern about this event?

— Where and how do I *start* to address this problem?

— What is preventing me from acting?

— What will help me to get started?

— Where do I find the resources I need (internal and external)?

9. Self-Disclosure — Self-disclosure quite simply means that we as crisis ministers disclose personal information about ourselves to the people in crisis. Although this skill is usually limited in other types of counseling, the crisis minister has more freedom to share here. The rules of self-disclosure still hold: Share for the benefit of the person in crisis, and be brief, to the point, and appropriate. However, the circumstances that invite this sharing are abundant in crisis ministry. People in crisis do not see options. We as crisis ministers can share having been in a similar position, maybe even in a similar situation, and how we were able to get through our crisis. The purpose of sharing is to serve as a model, to let them know that they are not the only ones to have felt at a loss and overwhelmed, and to present them with some possibilities for getting through their crisis. They will, of course, still need to choose and own their options.

10. Immediacy — Egan has three different types of immediacy:[6] overall relationship immediacy, event-focused immediacy, and self-involving statements (209–212). The one most appropriate to crisis ministry is *relationship immediacy*. As crisis ministers, many of the people we minister to will be known to us, and we will therefore be able to draw upon our knowledge of them through our previous relationship with them. When we see them in crisis as frightened, insecure, overwhelmed, and unable to decide or go forward, we can remind them of the people we know them to be—decisive, competent, and capable. We can do this because of our *relationship* with them; therefore, what we say is backed up by credibility.

Principles and Conditions for Doing Crisis Ministry

Doing good crisis ministry assumes certain basic conditions and principles that are important to name. Douglas Puryear has listed eight principles (20–21):

1. Immediate Response — A person, family, or community in crisis needs our immediate attention and intervention.

2. Active Intervention and Action — The crisis minister is a person of assertiveness, action, foresight, and planning.

3. Limited Goal — Crisis counseling differs from grief and long-term counseling. Crisis counseling works to get people back to precrisis states with some new learning and growth.

4. Hopeful Expectations — The crisis minister is a person of hope who brings that hope to the people in crisis. The crisis minister expects and conveys a hopeful and hope-filled outcome.

5. Support — Crisis ministers walk with the person in crisis; we also convey the message of God being with us in crisis.

6. Focused Problem-Solving — Crisis counseling focuses on naming the crisis event and helping the people resolve the problem or plan for strategies to change the situation. Crisis counseling is present oriented, short term, and directive.

7. Self-Esteem — The crisis minister is aware of how the people in crisis view themselves and works to protect and enhance the self-images, which may be damaged throughout the crisis process.

8. Independence — Crisis ministers help as much as is necessary and then step back. We help the person in crisis to act, and then we encourage independence.

To Puryear's principles, I would add four of my own:

1. Faith — Crisis ministers are by definition people of faith—faith in God, in ourselves, and in the people in crisis. This faith is a belief that the good that happens in the crisis caring comes not only from good skills and perseverance but is also because of God's presence and healing power.

2. Resilience — The crisis minister is a person of great resilience, able to hear stories of great personal pain and even of mass evil and destruction, without succumbing to pessimism or despair.

3. Concreteness — Crisis ministers are grounded in reality; we are pragmatic and concrete. We approach crises from a solvable, commonsense perspective. We deal with the concrete facts of a situation and the concrete steps necessary for change.

4. Referral — The crisis minister believes in the importance of referral and does not hesitate to make referrals to other helping agencies and other helping professionals.

Finally, it is important to recognize that in order to do (good) crisis ministry, certain *conditions* are necessary (1–4 are McGee's [323–324]; 5–8 are mine):

1. place

2. availability

3. mobility

4. flexibility of procedure

All of these conditions define good crisis ministry as ministry that is willing to meet people where they are, both literally and figuratively. Crisis ministers are located in an accessible place, and if we are not, we are willing to move and make ourselves available to the person or people in crisis. We are also willing to adapt our style and techniques to meet the needs of those in crisis. To these conditions I would add:

5. centeredness

6. self-belief (confidence)

7. humility

8. preparedness

Three of McGee's conditions are external factors; my additions (and McGee's fourth condition) are more internal factors related to the crisis minister. In order for good crisis ministry to occur, the crisis minister must be a centered, confident, humble, flexible, and knowledgeable person who is willing to adapt, move, and be available.

5

Crisis and the Community: Teaching, Preaching, Worship, Prayer, and Prophecy

The term *pastoral care* has been defined both broadly as the care pastors or faith communities provide for each other throughout their lifetime and specifically as the healing, sustaining, guiding, reconciling, nurturing, and liberating provided by representative Christian persons. In recent times, pastoral care has become most closely associated with the concept of *diakonia* (service) and has been linked with pastoral counseling. I prefer to return to a broad concept of pastoral care that includes *kerygma* (proclamation) and *koinonia* (community relationship with God). This broader definition also honors the priestly tradition, with an emphasis on worship, and the prophetic tradition, with an emphasis on justice and morality (Gerkin 25). This chapter will address how crisis care involves pastoral care as teaching, preaching, worship, prayer, and prophecy.

Teaching

The best time to teach crisis care is *before* a crisis occurs. Although we do not always know *exactly when* illness, death, divorce, school problems, or job loss will occur, we know that they *will* occur *sometime.* In order to prepare for crisis events, we need to teach our faith communities through what is called *primary prevention* strategies. The concept of primary prevention assumes that we can be *proactive* and *intentional* in helping to keep certain crises from happening in the first place. So although we can't totally prevent AIDS, teenage pregnancy, battering, bad parenting, or rape, we can provide educational programs to help educate about and prevent their occurrence. Since we know that certain events are *likely* to evoke crisis reactions, we can *anticipate* these events and work to *minimize* the crisis reaction and even promote growth (Hoff 22). By knowing who is at risk, we can target our teaching of information, skills, and resources for coping in these situations. Examples of high-risk situations include surgery, physical disability, and illness (health); fatal accident, suicide, and homicide (unexpected death); rape, domestic violence, and incarceration (crime); fire, flood, hurricane, airline crash, and nuclear accident (natural and human-made disasters); invasion, taking of hostages (war and related acts); economic setbacks, relocation, and divorce (family and economic) (Slaikeu 66–73). For teens, problems that are likely to evoke crisis reactions include drugs, sex, pregnancy, AIDS, peer pressure, school problems, crime and gangs, and getting along with parents (Weaver, Preston, and Jerome 19). Knowing *who* is likely to be at risk and *when* we can offer information and resources will bolster the ability to cope. This will better help individuals, families, and communities get through crisis.

A few ways to do this include:

— *Removing or changing the hazardous factors*. Example: By teaching the importance of immunizations and providing the means to get immunized, we can help prevent disease and its accompanying crises.

— *Reducing exposure to hazardous factors*. Example: By teaching about HIV infection, we can help reduce the spread of AIDS and its accompanying crises.

— *Reducing vulnerability by increasing our ability to deal with challenges*. Example: By preparing for life transitions such as marriage, retirement, and moving, we are less likely to experience these transitions as crises (Hoff 22–23).

As *pastoral ministers* we are in a unique position in relation to crisis teaching. We can teach about war, death, loss of faith, and economic setbacks in Bible-study groups and Scripture workshops. For instance, we can highlight different people in Scripture who faced and survived crises. We can do this *before* particular crises hit our faith community and the people in it. By learning how *others* — both individuals and communities — coped with crisis, we will be better equipped to face our *own* crises. We can also bring in consultants and provide programs on more secular topics such as planning for old age, loss, death, and grief. Or we can provide programs that educate on a secular and social level and on a religious and church level. Examples of these types of programs might include: How should our church respond to the AIDS pandemic? How does our faith affect how we view illness and death? How does an all-good God allow suffering in the world? Teaching allows us to address crisis events and reactions *before* they occur. Teaching also embraces what Joseph Jeter calls the *third theological affirmation in response to crisis: promise* — teaching that God is with us now and always (34–38).

Preaching

Jeter also lists *preaching* as part of the *third theological affirmation of promise* (ibid.). It is in crisis preaching that the pastoral minister acknowledges and names the crisis and moves to God's hopeful word (ibid. 105). Certainly preaching can and *should* also be done as part of *primary prevention* — before the congregation is in crisis. The Sunday sermon or homily[1] can and should be used to talk about the life, death, and resurrection of Jesus Christ in relation to experiencing and getting through crises *when the preacher or community is not in crisis.* This is less anxiety provoking for the preacher and the congregation than preaching in the *midst* of a crisis. Preachers should be reminded to do this more often.

Pastoral care through preaching will most often be done in the *midst* of a crisis, whether public, personal, or congregational. If public, the preaching will address such things as the outbreak of war, a terrorist attack, or a flood or hurricane that caused damage and loss of life locally. If congregational, the preaching will be about something that has affected this *particular* congregation, such as the death or removal of a pastor, or a plan to close or cluster the congregation; if personal, it will be preaching in the midst of the preacher's personal crisis, such as death, divorce, or illness (ibid. 14).

Jeter suggests a structure for crisis preaching that can help us write and preach sermons or homilies during crisis (104):

— Acknowledge the concern(s) of the person or people. (A)

— Engage the tension between the situation and the Gospel by speaking a word of hope when things seem hopeless and proclaiming the good news over evil and suffering. (GH)

— Suggest a new direction. (F)

Jeter actually builds his model from Jones's (chapter 3 ABC model), overlaying the ABC model, the truth of the situation, with what he calls DEF, the truth of the sermon, and GH, the engagement of the tension of situation and Gospel.

All of this is done in the context of a loving community of faith.

Jeter lists key principles of preaching in crisis (75–94):

— Deciding whether a crisis exists — for the pastor or the congregation

— Naming the monster — giving voice to what has evoked the crisis reaction

— Lamenting — using Scripture (Book of Lamentations), or writing an original prayer of lamentation

— Seeing and believing in biblical wagons (Genesis 45:27) — examples of God's wagons today include Scripture, the Eucharist, the cross, and the sermon

— Needing constancy — drawing from great homilies of the past, such as Chrysostom's *Homilies on the Statues,* which teach us the importance of continuity; the present crisis is probably part of a deeper, ongoing crisis

— Calling for courage — preaching is challenging and the preacher needs courage to witness to the truth

Lee Ramsey has some helpful guidelines for crisis preaching. He reminds us that the *primary* aim of crisis preaching is to *sustain* the congregation; the *secondary* pastoral intent is to *guide* the congregation to a *beginning* theological understanding of the event (180–181). These two functions are two of the primary functions of pastoral care. The preacher is in tune with her congregation and their needs, even if she is not where they are at in relation to a crisis event. For instance, the congregation may be in crisis over an event, such as the firing of the local public school principal; however, the pastoral minister may *not* have a crisis reaction to this event. Still it is up to the pastoral minister to orient the homily or sermon to the community's needs (ibid. 180) and to give voice to the community's concerns (ibid. 179). The preacher is teacher, preacher, theologian, prophet, *and counselor.* In all these roles, he or she provides pastoral care for the faith community.

In a crisis the world as we know it may be shattered. Our values, worldview, and faith may be shaken to their core. Therese Rando, a clinical psychologist, would call this a blow to our *assumptive world*. The assumptive world is both global and specific. In a crisis, specifically in a crisis involving a death, a person's *global assumptions* are shattered; for example, the person's belief that God protects the young, the good, or the innocent is negated in the death of a child. A person's *specific assumptions* are also shattered; for example, the belief that *my* child will always be with *me* is invalidated (Rando 50–53). The preacher needs to be aware of this assault and also aware of *who* makes up the congregation and *what* their theology is. The crisis preacher must know and have a relationship with his community. Crisis preaching is about naming the monster (Jeter), but it is also about naming the sin (Taylor). It is about encouraging congregations to stay in the grave for a while as they reflect on and try to understand the death, loss, or devastation that has befallen them. We are an Easter people, so we know that resurrection is assured; but we must first endure the grief of Holy Saturday.

Both Taylor and Walter Brueggemann point out the importance of using metaphor in crisis preaching. For Brueggemann, the primary metaphor for crisis preaching is the concept of *exile* in the Hebrew Scriptures. He suggests the metaphor of exile as a way to help understand the present faith situation in the U.S. Roman Catholic Church as well as a model for a new ecclesiology for the church (Brueggemann, "Preaching" 9). As a church in exile, we need to grieve our losses; we are like children without mothers (ibid. 13–15). We are in danger of becoming despondent because we have lost our treasured symbols of God's presence (ibid. 16–19). Brueggemann suggests a number of ways the preacher and worship leader can lead their exiled people. As preachers we need to name and face the loss (crisis) and address our pain to God (ibid. 31). This is done in the crisis homily using lament resources such as the Book of Lamentations, Isaiah, psalms of lament, and scriptural words of assurance (Romans 4:17; Jeremiah 31–34; Ezekiel 37:13–14) as the background for, if not the actual text of, the homily. More will be said about lament as prayer and worship in the section on prayer.

Finally, I would like to suggest an outline or guide for crisis preaching:[2]

Determine whether and what type of crisis exists.

— Is this a crisis for the preacher, individuals in the community, the entire community, or the world?

— Listen to ourselves (inner voice), others (dialogue), and God (prayer and Scripture).

Name the crisis (the monster, the sin).

— Clearly identify and define what event or experience we are reacting to.

Assess where we (the preacher and the community) are in relation to the crisis.

— Assess where we are *subjectively* — in relation to our feelings and values.

— Assess where we are *objectively* — what is causing or contributing to the crisis — *economically, socially, and psychologically.*

— Assess where we are in relation to the crisis — at the beginning, the middle, or the end.

Reflect theologically on the crisis event and our reaction to it.

— Pray, read Scripture, and look to church tradition and teachings.

— Ask where God is in this situation; discern what God is asking of us as preachers and as communities of faith.

Prepare the homily.

— Name the crisis — facts and feelings.

— Name where we feel God's presence or absence.

— Look at what metaphors Scripture offers us.

— Ask ourselves, are we lamenting, consoling, challenging, or encouraging action? This will depend on the type of crisis and where we are in relation to the crisis.

— Name any questions that remain.

— Offer ways to cope.

— Provide a word of hope.

— Keep the homily short and to the point.

Worship

Preaching is, of course, done in the context of worship, which Jeter names as the *theological affirmation of remembrance* or hope in the past (28). Jeter names five principles of worship in crisis: Worship offers us sanctuary, familiarity, help, prayer, and witness to our beliefs (67–72). Worship services in times of crisis need to address the crisis, in such places as the homily and the prayer of the faithful, but also need to remain essentially the same to provide familiarity, continuity, and safety. Presiders and preachers should spend more time and care in preparing and in reading their own pulses as well as the pulse of their communities.

Robert Hater has suggested five guidelines for liturgy that may be particularly applied during times of crisis (13–14):

1. *Liturgies need to pay attention to rites of passage and pivotal moments (which may be crisis moments) in a parishioner's life or in the life of the community.* Rites of passage include birth, marriage, sickness, and death, which may be developmental turning points (crises) and may be situational crises. Hater writes that the presider, the liturgical ministers, and the community need to connect the liturgy with the needs of the community. The homily is one venue for doing this; the prayer of the faithful is another way; the liturgical ministers as representatives of the community are another venue. How they welcome, support, and respond to the individual congregant or congregation's needs is essential.

2. *Liturgies need to celebrate core realities.* Music, gestures, and the homily need to address the core realities of the community: birth and death and important moments in life. Being a welcoming and hospitable community is also essential before, during, and after a crisis. This welcoming and hospitable attitude needs to be reflected in all aspects of the community life, especially in the liturgy. When hospitality spreads throughout the parish, the liturgy is naturally

welcoming, and welcoming liturgies are more likely to be experienced as connecting with core realities.

3. *Liturgies need to be functional and to address core realities.* Ritual requires both structure and spontaneity. The structure of the liturgy needs to remain faithful to the functional dimensions of the liturgy; the paschal mystery is always proclaimed and celebrated, even during a crisis. The liturgy needs also to be spontaneous and flexible to respond to pastoral needs. This does not mean improvisation, but it does mean connecting the liturgy with the core realities of the lives of the community; it also means connecting the liturgy with the *context* of what is happening in the community, both internally and externally.

4. *Liturgies need to celebrate real-life experiences.* Homilies need to respond to what is going on in the world, in the worshiping community, and in the lives of individual congregants, such as baptisms and weddings. Music, words, and gestures need to address, reflect, and connect to the needs of our particular community. We need to be aware of who makes up our community and where they are in relation to celebrations and concerns. We need to adapt gestures, music, the homily, and the prayer of the faithful to respond to needs.

5. *Liturgies are opportunities to establish and support Catholic identity.* For Roman Catholics, every Eucharist is a remembrance, affirmation, and celebration of core meanings that define us as Roman Catholic: the life, death, and resurrection of Jesus Christ and his ongoing presence with us in the Eucharist and the gathered community of faith. Liturgies during crisis need to take the crisis into account and respond to the needs of the people without losing touch with the proclamation and celebration of the paschal mystery

The previous section mentioned one place in the liturgy or the worship service where crises can be addressed — the homily. In Hater's five points, other possibilities were alluded to: liturgical gestures, music, and words. I would like to focus on the general intercessions (prayer of the faithful or, in Protestant traditions, cares and concerns), in which crises can be particularly addressed. This section is written from a Roman Catholic perspective but may be adapted for other traditions.

Prayer of the Faithful[3]

The *Roman Missal* gives a lot of latitude in the writing of the prayer of the faithful. The prayer consist of three parts:

1. An invitation (addressed to the people and said by the presider)

2. Intentions (addressed to the people and said by the deacon or lay reader)

3. Concluding prayer (addressed to God and said by the presider)

In the *invitation,* the reason for the prayers may be linked to the readings and the prayer is brief: "Come let us pray ...."

The *intentions* consist of four parts:

1. The reader asks the people to pray for an intention: "For all who ...."

2. The people pray in silence.

3. The reader invites an invocation from the people: "We pray to the Lord ...."

4. The people respond with the invocation: "We pray to the Lord ...."

The *content* of the intentions can address or reflect:

— The needs of the church, local and universal

— Public authorities or the salvation of the world

— Those oppressed by any need, such as disaster or war

— The needs of the local community, such as sickness or death

The *concluding prayer* is said by the presider and addressed to God the Creator, the first person of the Trinity:

1. It is addressed to God.

2. God is praised for who God is or what God has done.

3. God is asked to hear our prayers.

4. The prayer is concluded through Christ or in Christ's name.

5. The people give their assent by responding Amen.

It is in the intentions read by a deacon or lay reader that particular concerns of the congregation — including personal, public, and congregational crisis (Jeter 14) — can be addressed.

Prayer

One type of prayer that is particularly appropriate in times of crisis and loss is the lament, particularly psalms of lament. In Scripture there are a number of psalms of lament — individual, communal, and penitential — found in the Book of Psalms. These readings may form a significant part of a worship service, or they may be incorporated into a service. Walter Brueggemann categorizes the psalms of lament as *psalms of disorientation* — disarray, anguish, hurt, and suffering. Examples of this type of psalm are psalms 13, 35, 74, 86, 109, and 130. These psalms of disorientation need to be seen in the context of *psalms of orientation* — tranquility, happiness, and safety (psalms 1, 8, 33, 37, 131, and 145) — and *psalms of new orientation* — songs of belief in God in times of distress (psalms 29, 34, 40, 65, 93, 97, and 124) (Brueggemann, *Message*). Times of crisis, life, loss, and grief have a cycle and the psalms can and should be prayed during all parts of the crisis cycle (precrisis, during crisis, and after crisis). These psalms can be used in corporate worship services but can also be prayed by individuals or as part of a group prayer.

The word *lament* is sometimes confused with the word *complain,* and many of us today want to avoid complaining to God. Yet, to lament is *more* than to complain. If I cry out to God and rail against God, it is because I have a belief in God and a strong relationship with God. Theologically, lament assumes there is a God who will and must hear because that is what God does; psychologically, lament assumes that we are helped in our suffering when we express our pain (Karaban, "Isaiah" 30).

The classic psalm of lament has elements of the following six parts (Brueggemann, "Foreword" x–xii):

1. God is named, often intimately.

2. A complaint is made.

3. A petition is made.

4. The complaint and petition are repeated and expressed in extreme terms.

5. A request is added to a petition, such as vengeance against the enemy.

6. Anger and protest are spent, and rejoicing and praise are voiced.

We see a similar formula and faith expressed in other Scripture passages, most notably in the Book of Job, when Moses petitions God (Exodus 32:11–14; Numbers 11:11–15), and in the Book of Jeremiah (11:18–12:6; 12:1–6; 15:10–21; 17:14–18; 18:19–23; 20:7–13; 20:14–18). Scripture, then, is replete with individuals and communities calling upon God in anguish and pain. In lament we see faithful and faith-filled people cry out in pain to God. This crying out involves trust, faith, courage, and love (Karaban, "Isaiah" 30), and it is in complaining to God that faith is affirmed and solace is found.

We may also write psalms and prayers of lament, just as Ann Weems wrote fifty personal lament psalms in response to the sudden death of her twenty-one-year-old son. Writing personal psalms of lament may make up part of the ritual that forms part of our getting through crisis. An example of a psalm of lament written in response to crisis appears in chapter 6.

Prophecy

As pastoral ministers we are called to be prophetic. One definition of pastoral care is that it takes on issues of justice and morality (Gerkin 29). The prophetic leader cares for the people and for the tradition that gives them a common identity (ibid.). One definition of pastoral counseling is that it has a prophetic dimension; it goes beyond the counseling relationship to the systems of injustice and oppression that cause and contribute to pain (Oates, *Pastoral*). This prophetic dimension of our ministry is done not only through our counseling but also through preaching, teaching, worship, and prayer. It is the common thread that connects and permeates our ministry. It is fueled by compassion, justice, hope, and vision.

I have pointed out how discernment is about understanding how our piece of the vision relates to God's vision (Karaban, *Responding* 2). We come to know our piece of the vision through the process of discerning God's call in our life. In relation to crisis care and our prophetic role as pastoral leaders, I would like to define *vision* further as being able to see what is invisible (Premnath 183). Visions are both collective and individual; the individual prophet addresses the collective experience of dissonance that she perceives (ibid.186). It is the ability to be visionary that allows the prophet to free feelings that have not yet been expressed (ibid. 187). It is in the midst of acute crisis and hopelessness that visions grow (ibid. 188). The prophet helps the person in crisis form a new consciousness that is alternative to the dominant belief (Brueggemann, *Prophetic* 44). She calls upon and uses the language of *prophetic imagination* (ibid. 46) to cut through the pain, disillusionment, and dissonance. The prophetic perspective brings us beyond the one-on-one ministry that crisis care (counseling) often involves to caring for communities through challenging their behaviors and even their beliefs. A prophetic perspective assumes a willingness to be compassionate and just. To be compassionate, or to love with justice, means allowing God's gift of anger to flow (Clarke 182). Both compassion and justice are built upon hope and upon a commitment to changing systems that perpetuate oppression, death, destruction, and poverty (Karaban, *Responding* 115). We act with justice and compassion based on hope that we both find within and offer to those to whom we minister (ibid. 115).

Part 2

Cases

Guidelines for Part 2

The next four chapters will present case material on the following crisis situations:

Chapter 6: Suicide

Chapter 7: Loss and Death

Chapter 8: Violence

Chapter 9: Community Disaster

Each chapter will use the following format to present and analyze the case:

1. Description of Event (vignette including the role of the crisis minister)

2. Assessment, Analysis, and Response (subjective: identification of feelings evoked; objective: identification of type of crisis, skills used, and model followed)

3. Understanding the Crisis in a Broader Context (background information; issues and concerns for the crisis minister)

4. Theological Reflection and Resources (theological themes, scriptural references, ritual, prayer, or homily)

If a case is based on a real situation, it has been altered to protect the identity of those involved. Otherwise, the case is made up from the author's imagination and experience.

Case studies are as much about the crisis minister who presents the case as they are about the person, family, or community in the case. It is my belief that we present cases for further analysis and reflection because we want to be better ministers and to give better crisis caring.

6

Suicide

1. Description of Event

Vignette

The call came at a time when I wasn't supposed to be at home, as so often happens. My daughter answered the phone.

R = Roslyn

D = Daughter

J = Joan

R: Who is it?

D1: She says it is Joan—from work.

Joan has never called me at home. We have a cordial work relationship, but are not friends outside work. It is ten o'clock on Sunday morning and I am usually at church right now. It is only by chance – or providence – that I am at home.

R1: Joan, it's Roslyn.

J1: Roslyn, I don't know who else to call. My son's best friend at college was just found dead—by a gunshot wound to his head. It was a suicide. My son is going crazy. He can't believe it. I can't either. Joe was with Sean a few days ago. He says Sean sounded okay, even cheerful. Sean is such a nice kid. How can I help Joe? What can I say? How could God allow this to happen?

R2: I am so sorry, Joan. I will do what I can to walk you through this. It must be very difficult for you and Joe being so far away from each other. Tell me more about what happened.

J2: I still don't know exactly. Just that Sean is dead and Joe is beside himself.

R3: Is anyone with Joe?

J3: Yes, the RA is with everyone, and they have called in a crisis counselor and a chaplain.

R4: What do you think Joe needs most right now?

J4: I think he wants me to be there with him and I am considering going—it's a long way away.

R5: Let's talk about that in a bit. Right now, let's see if we can address the immediate needs for both Joe and you.

J5: Okay.

R6: Let's start with Joe. What does he need most right now?

J6: I think he needs to not be alone.

R7: Does he have someone with him who will stay with him?

J7: I know his roommate is there, and I will make sure that Chad stays with him. He also has a cell phone, and I can check in with him.

R8: You may want to be more specific about this. Let him know you will check in with him every two hours and that you will be available with your cell phone if he needs you before you check in. You can also talk with Chad to make sure he is okay and able to stay with Joe. Is there anyone else that Joe can talk to?

J8: Actually, Joe is quite close to the chaplain, Father Bill. I think it would help him to talk with him.

R9: Can you also talk with Father Bill about your concerns about Joe?

J9: Yes, I can call him.

R10: Joan, you know Joe, how do you think he is handling this? Do you have any concerns for his safety?

J10: What do you mean?

R11: Sometimes after a suicide, friends feel so bad they may have thoughts of hurting themselves. You will need to ask Joe specifically about this. If he is suicidal, you need to make sure he is not alone and that he has people there he can talk with to help him though his pain.

J11: I can do that. They were so close. I worry about how he will react.

R12: Joan, let me summarize where we are so far. After we talk, you will call Joe and make sure he is with someone. You will talk to both Father Bill and Chad. You will let Joe know that you are available by cell phone and that you will check on him every two hours. You will let him know it is important that he stay with someone and that he let them or you know if he has any ideas of harming himself. Once you hear Joe's response to all this, you can then decide whether you need to drive down there to be with him today or whether that can wait. Now let's talk about you a bit.

J12: Okay.

R13: Where are you with all of this?

J13: Feeling a bit better now that I have talked with you and I know some things to do.

R14: Do you have anyone there with you?

J14: Yes, my husband, Paul, is here and will go with me if I decide that is what we need to do.

R15: Is there anyone or anything else that can help support you right now?

J15: I think I won't come into work tomorrow, no matter if I go or not. That would help me be free for Joe and give me time to process this. Do you know any support groups I can call for helping us all get though this?

R16: Yes, I know of a few. I will need to find the numbers. I will call you back later this afternoon. Is three okay? May I have your cell phone number to reach you?

J16: Yes, I will have it on—333-7777.

R17: How are you doing now, Joan?

J17: Still in shock, but a bit better.

R18: Joan, earlier in the conversation you asked how could God do this. Is that something you want to talk more about now?

J18: No, that can wait. I can't really go there right now.

R19: We can talk more about that later. For now, I will keep you, Chad, Joe, and Sean's family in my prayers.

J19: Thanks, Roslyn. I am so glad that you were there.

R20: I will help in any way I can, Joan. I'll call you at three.

My Role

This phone call happened over a fifteen-minute period on a Sunday morning. Joan is a coworker, but we have never talked on this level before. Because of the nature of the call, I see myself as her *crisis caregiver* and quickly fall into that role.

2. Assessment, Analysis, and Response

— Subjective: identification of feelings evoked

— Objective: identification of type of crisis, skills used, and model followed

Subjective Analysis

Feelings Evoked

I was very *surprised* to get a phone call from Joan. I *hoped* I could help. I knew she expected a lot from me. That made me a bit *uncomfortable*. I *hoped* I could live up to her expectations. I was *worried* about Joe and his state of mind. I kept thinking, You're not even supposed to be home; you must be here for a purpose. Help her! I felt *pressured* yet *calm*. I really felt God's presence in my being there and being able to remain so calm.

As the conversation progressed, I remained *calm* and was able to help. Part of me resented getting a call at home on a Sunday morning from someone I didn't know very well, with a serious problem. I asked myself, Why me? Why now? Do I always have to be a counselor? This will be reflected on in section 4, Theological Reflection.

Objective Analysis

Type of Crisis

This was a **situational crisis.** The *hazardous event* for Joe was Sean's suicide and the *precipitating event* was his being told of his friend's death. For Joan, the *hazardous event* was Sean's suicide; the *precipitating event* was Joe's reaction and phone call to her. This is also a complicated grief situation because it is the sudden, traumatic, and violent death of a young person. Suicide is one of the most complicated deaths to get through.[1] The survivors are in the first phase of grief: shock and disbelief. They are questioning how this could have happened and where was God in all of this.

Model and Skills: CARING

Connect — Whether or not a situational crisis exists, and in this case it did, I follow the first guideline (Connect): Center myself; attend to person; be present physically, emotionally, and spiritually. This is a bit more difficult over the phone, but I let Joan know I am listening to her and am there for her. I immediately focus on the conversation at hand, giving Joan my full attention. I say a silent prayer for guidance and wisdom. Internally, I shift into my *professional counselor mode* and out of my casual, Sunday, relax-at-home mode. I go into another room where we can talk privately and focus only on the conversation at hand. I try to convey interest and concern through my tone of voice.

Skill: Presence (R1)

Assess — I internally do an Assessment of the situation being presented. I ask myself, Does a situational crisis exist? Suicide is a sudden, unexpected life event that is evoking in Joe and Joan a possible crisis reaction. There is some *crisis behavior* and *crisis cognition* displayed; they are both overwhelmed and don't know what to do next.

I listen to see if the persons (both Joe and Joan) are *functioning.* Are either of them *suicidal* or *homicidal*? Neither appears to be suicidal or homicidal. I ask Joan about Joe later on in the conversation (R11). This will be something to watch in days to come.

I look for the *main concern.* For Joe, the main concern is not knowing what to do in response to his friend's death. For Joan, the main concern is how best to respond to her son's distress.

I identify *resources.* Joe has friends, a chaplain, an RA, a crisis counselor, and Mom and Dad. Joan has me, her husband, the telephone, and places to contact for more help. It is too early to know if faith or a worshiping community will be part of their resources.

Skills: Assessment, Empathy, Probes, Information Questions

— Empathy: R2 ("It must be very difficult for you and Joe being so far away from each other.")

— Assessment (gathering information): R2 ("Tell me more about what happened"); R3, R4, R6, R7, R8 ("Is there anyone else Joe can talk to?"); R8, R9, R10, R13, R14, R15, R16 (last part)

— Probes and Information Questions: R2 (last part), R3, R4, R5, R6, R7, R8 (last question), R9, R10, R13, R14, R15, R16 (last part), R17, R18

Respond — The initial response is made through Presence and Assessment and is continued through providing Information, Summarizing, and ordering and prioritizing what happened and where the person is in relation to the crisis event.

Skills: Assessment, Empathy, Summary, Leverage

— Assessment and Empathy were covered under Assessment earlier.

— Leverage can be seen in R4, R5, end of R12 and R19.

— Summary can be found in R12 and the beginning of R18.

Intervene — This consisted of actively continuing to intervene in the crisis by setting up a concrete *action plan* (both short- and long-term), and by giving the person direct feedback and information on where she is at and what her options are.

Skills: Information Sharing, Self-Disclosure, Immediacy

— Information Sharing: R8, R11 (plan), R16, R20.

— The beginning of R16 may be called Self-Disclosure.

— Immediacy was used in the beginning of R10.

Network — As crisis caregivers we always need to remember
that we are not alone in helping people in crisis. We need to access
and summarize resources for those in crisis. We need to remind
ourselves that *we* also may need resources, such as a supervisor
or spiritual guide. As crisis *ministers* we need to remember that we
are not alone; God is always part of who we are and what we do.[2]

Skills: Information Sharing, Referral

- Information is shared in R8, R11, R16, R20.

- Referral is mentioned in R16.

Get Together — This is part of a follow-up, setting a specific time to
check in to see how the person in crisis is doing.

Skills: Information Sharing

- Information was shared in R8, R11, R16, R20.

- R16 and R20 are specific in how the follow-up (get together)
  will occur.

Summary of Skills Used

R1 — Presence
R2 — Sympathy, Empathy, Open Probe (Assessment)
R3 — Information Question (Assessment)
R4 — Open Probe (Assessment), Leverage
R5 — Probe, Leverage
R6 — Open Probe (Assessment)
R7 — Information Question (Assessment)
R8 — Information Sharing (formulating a plan); Information
  Question (Assessment)
R9 — Information Question (Assessment)
R10 — Immediacy, Open Probe, Information Question (Assessment)
R11 — Information Sharing (Plan)
R12 — Summary, Leverage
R13 — Open Probe (Assessment)
R14 — Information Question (Assessment)
R15 — Information Question (Assessment)
R16 — Self-Disclosure, Information Sharing Referral and Follow-up,
  Information Question
R17 — Open Probe (Assessment)
R18 — Summary, Information Question (Assessment)

R19 — Leverage, Summary
R20 — Information Sharing (Follow-up)

3. Understanding the Crisis in a Broader Context

Background Information

Suicide is one of the most complicated losses to grieve. It falls under the category of *disenfranchised grief* (Doka) because it is a loss that is a socially unsanctioned death with a stigma (Karaban, *Complicated* 36). Disenfranchised grievers often lack support and are unable to share emotions openly, making it harder to grieve. A death by suicide is sudden, unanticipated, usually untimely, and often violent. Survivors often feel the death was preventable and thus must deal with more guilt and shame, more negativity, and more of a need to make sense of, or find meaning in the death. All of these factors contribute to classifying suicide as a complicated loss or difficult death (Karaban) and also contribute to evoking crisis reactions in the survivors.

It may be helpful to put Sean's death in a broader context. We know that he is part of a growing trend among young adults. Suicide is now the third leading cause of death among those aged fifteen to twenty-four, and these deaths most often take place at home between the hours of midnight and three a.m.; males are more likely to die from suicide, because they choose violent means, but females are four times more likely to attempt suicide; white males are at the highest risk for suicide and are two times more likely to commit suicide than African American males, though suicides among African Americans are increasing; hanging and firearms are common methods used by young, white males.[3]

There is much that can be done to *prevent* suicide, but this case is about working with survivors of suicide *after* the death has occurred. It is important for the crisis caregiver to understand the *distinctiveness* of suicidal grief.

Suicidal grief has its own unique grieving process.

The first phase of grief — shock and denial — is particularly difficult for the suicide survivor. The suicide survivor must be encouraged to name the death as a suicide — as difficult as that may be — or the crisis cannot be worked through, nor the grieving proceed. The shock of the death may be greater because it is sudden, traumatic, unexpected, violent, and untimely. The crisis caregiver will need to be prepared for the intensity of the shock reaction of the survivors.

Grief feelings of survivors are more intense, and we need to encourage expression of these feelings.

Survivors of suicide experience intense feelings of anger and guilt. If these feelings are denied or not expressed, they may be directed inwardly toward the survivor, leading to self-destructive thoughts and behaviors. They may also be directed outwardly toward others; suicide survivors may project their anger or guilt onto a person or agency, blaming them for their loved one's death. This projection may result in increased aggressive, even hostile behavior. Feelings of depression, hopelessness, and self-pity are also intensified.

Suicidal grief can lead to distorted or chronic grieving.

Distorted grief is an exaggeration or distortion of anger or guilt due to an inability on the griever's part to react to the loss and express feelings of anger and guilt. Suicidal grief may also become *chronic grief,* which is a continued manifestation of intense grief reactions that usually only occur early in the grieving process. Suicide survivors are unable to let go of the person who has died and get on with life because of the manner of the death and an inability to make sense of the death. Distorted and chronic grief are two types of complicated grief that will take additional help and support and will require referral to a professional grief counselor.[4]

Given the complexities surrounding suicide, many of us would prefer *not* to deal with it. Yet as crisis caregivers, we will probably be one of the *first* helpers contacted when a person hears of a suicidal death (as in this case). Referral will come later in the process.

Issues and Concerns for the Crisis Minister

Suicide can evoke a crisis reaction in caregivers.

Not only is suicide one of the hardest deaths for the survivor, it is one of the hardest deaths for the crisis caregiver to respond to. The details of the death can be violent, even gruesome, and the reactions of the survivors can be extreme. As crisis caregivers we must call on patience, compassion, and faith to remain calm and confident as we respond to survivors. We may ourselves need to debrief with a colleague or supervisor as we may struggle with our own feelings and faith questions in the midst of a suicide. In this case, most of my issues and concerns were theological in nature and will be addressed in the next section.

4. Theological Reflection and Resources

As a *pastoral* crisis caregiver responding to Joan, I identified a number of theological *themes or issues* that emerged in our conversation. Joan asked the question, "How could God allow this to happen?" On the surface, I was able to respond to her by allowing her to *ask* the question without feeling compelled to give a theological treatise in reply. This reaction followed the three-question principle first set out by Mitchell and Anderson (171) that we often ask *why God* three times in grief. I propose that we also do this when we are in crisis. The *first* time we ask the question out of anger and rage, and we do not really expect an answer. This is how Joan asked the question, and I was able to let her express her anger at God without feeling I needed to defend or explain God's action or inaction. I also did not feel compelled to share my image of God as one who does not *cause* our pain but who gives us free choice and then is with us when our choices, or our humanity, result in suffering and pain. Yet underneath my immediate response, there lurked another response that I did not express openly. Part of me wanted to respond, "I don't know, Joan. What kind of a God would do that?"

As I reflect on this encounter from a theological perspective, I continue to examine my *own* faith and my *own* beliefs about God. I do not believe God causes bad things to happen to good people, but I do believe that, as God's created, we have the right to rail at

God. This is part of my Judeo-Christian tradition, and I need only go to the book of Job or the psalms of lament to know that I am not alone in my pain or in my challenging God.

Joan never pursued the theological themes with me because I was more of a colleague to her. However, because of what her questions evoked in me, and because of who I am, I felt compelled to have a conversation with God and to express my anger, doubts, and concerns to God. The following psalm of lament is what developed:

> God, you know what it is like to
> lose a son.
> How could you allow any parent
> to endure that same pain?
> You have the power to stop a suicide —
> Why didn't you?
>
> Over and over I am asked why —
> I ask the same of you,
> Why, O Lord, Why must we suffer?
> Where are you in our despair?
>
> Yet even as I cry out to you
> in anger and pain,
> I feel your gentle, loving touch,
> and I stand still.
>
> So still I can hear what you have been whispering
> to me all along,
> I am with you and I share your pain,
> my beloved daughter.

A secondary theological issue for me as the caregiver is an ongoing one. As I reflected on what bothered me about this encounter, I realized I was left with some resentment about being called at home, on my day off, with such a dreadful situation. I asked God, "Why me? Why now?" Do I always have to be the minister or counselor wherever I go? Can't I just stay at home and read the paper sometime? This issue emerges for me often — at the supermarket, in aerobics class, on an airplane, or at my son's school. I wear no collar and am not ordained, and yet no matter where I go, I seem to have people approach me for help. How do they know who I am or what I do? Can't I just go buy a loaf of bread without hearing someone's life story or hearing about why they left the church? As I write this I know that I am exaggerating, and yet these encounters occur often. As I look at the many times this has happened, I realize that I *invite* people into my life. I let them know that I am safe, open, receptive, and available. Joan was able to call me because she knew I was a good listener and that I would be able to help her. I do not get called at home often and the times that I have received calls were extreme situations. When I responded to God's call to be a pastoral minister through the vocation of teaching and pastoral care and counseling, I knew that this would not be a nine-to-five job, but that it would be *who* I would *become.* I am a pastoral counselor and pastoral theologian, whether I am at home reading the paper, or on a plane traveling to visit my friend. It is *not* something I can or *want* to leave behind; it has become part of the very fabric of who I am and I *like* that others see me in this role, even when I am not behind a desk or in a classroom. Obviously, I need to watch that I am also cared for and ministered to, and I need to be able to buy groceries and watch soccer games without providing pastoral care to everyone present. But I have come to peace with *who* I am, and *what* I do, and I am truly thankful to God for my gifts and abilities that permeate every aspect of my life.

7

Loss and Death

Sometimes we find ourselves in crisis situations where we are not sure *what* our role is. The encounter I am describing lasted no longer than fifteen minutes, and I never again saw any of the people involved. Yet, the situation has remained etched in my heart and mind, and the questions and concerns raised from the encounter are ones I continue to reflect on. The analysis will be written from two perspectives: (1) from how it actually happened, and my involvement in it; and (2) from the perspective of the young priest and how he might have experienced what happened.

1. What Actually Happened: Description of Event

Vignette

A few months ago I was scheduled to teach a class in a rectory a few hours away from where I live. I arrived early and rang the doorbell. A young priest (male, early thirties, Caucasian, wearing clerical clothes, including collar) answered the door. I introduced myself and said that I was scheduled to teach a class there that night. He invited me in and we went up a set of stairs to a landing; he checked the schedule, indicating that there might be a problem. He came back and told me that the room I was scheduled to teach in was booked for another activity that night. The young priest (YP) went to get the pastor. While he was gone, the doorbell rang. I stood there wondering if I should answer the door, as it could be one of my students. I decided it might also *not* be my student, and it was probably not *proper* for me to answer the doorbell. I even wondered if it was *safe* for me to do so. The bell kept ringing. Finally, the young priest returned with the pastor (P) (Caucasian, male, sixties, also in clerical clothes). The pastor talked with me about the room conflict while the young priest went downstairs to answer the door. I was soon distracted by the conversation at the front door. I heard the voice of a young woman who was very upset.

W = Woman

YP = Young Priest

M = My Thoughts

W1: Can you help me, please?

M1: (Has she been attacked? She sounds desperate.)

YP1: What can I do for you?

W2: My baby has just died, and it is so hard!

M2: (That poor woman! My heart goes out to her. What will he say?)

YP2: Won't you come in?

W3: Yes, Father.

W4: Should I have had the baby baptized?

YP3: No, that was not necessary. We believe that the child is with God.

M3: (Was it a stillbirth? What happened? When? I have missed the details.)

W5: Should I name him?

YP4: That is up to you. You may find it helpful.

W6: It's so hard (*crying*).

M4: (Yes, tell me more.)

W7: Can I have a service?

YP5: Yes, that is possible.

W8: Could I have a reading from today's Gospel? It's something from Mark, but I don't remember what.

YP6: We can check on it. I will get the lectionary and we can look it up.

He leaves her for a moment to get the lectionary.

M5: (Why is he leaving her there alone? Is it so important to check the reading right now and not respond to her distress?)

Meanwhile, I was trying to address my problem. My students were arriving in minutes and there was no space for us in the rectory. The pastor did not *seem* to be aware of the conversation at the front door and was animatedly talking with me about the school I teach at (his former seminary), while his maintenance person was finding us a room at the school. I wanted to go down and talk with the woman at the door, but I felt *stuck* at the top of the stairs dealing with what seemed like the mundane task of finding a room. As I walked down the stairs to go to the school, I saw that the young woman was gone. I heard the young priest tell the pastor that she was with the female pastoral associate (FPA) who was there for a meeting and that the pastoral associate was helping the young woman plan a service.

My Role

I was there as a professor, not a counselor, yet I am also a trained grief therapist, pastoral counselor, and a mother. I was clear on what my role was, but I was also aware of the other hats I wear and I believed that I could be of help because of my other roles.

2. Assessment, Analysis, and Response

— Subjective: identification of feelings evoked

— Objective: identification of type of crisis, skills used, and model followed

Subjective Analysis

Feelings Evoked

I felt *torn.* My heart was with the woman at the door and my *desire* was to *help* her. Although I knew I couldn't take away her pain, I felt I could help her through her initial shock and despair. I kept responding to her in my head, wanting to reach out to her. I actually felt an *ache* in my heart. One part of me wished I had answered the door. Another part of me thought, "It is not your place; trust that another can help." I felt *sad* and *startled.* I felt *responsible* to my class, for finding them space and meeting with them. Yet I also felt the young woman's crisis took precedence over my noncrisis situation. I felt *relieved* when I heard that the young woman was sitting and talking with another female minister.

Objective Analysis

Type of Crisis

This was a **situational crisis** that may also be classified as a *sociocultural crisis.* The death of the woman's child was unpredicted and unanticipated. It was also *interruptive,* having an external origin. Because there were significant contextual issues involved, particularly gender, it may also be classified as *sociocultural.* The fact that the person in crisis was female and a mother affected how she perceived her crisis, society's response to it, and the helping relationship with a male, celibate priest. These sociocultural (contextual) issues will be looked at from my perspective and the perspective of the young priest.

Model and Skills: Hoff's Four-Step Model (Assess, Plan, Intervene, and Follow-up)

This event occurred *before* I had developed my CARING model of crisis intervention, so I followed the model I was most familiar with: Assess, Plan, Intervene, and Follow-up. Much of my response focused on the first part of this model, *assessing* whether the woman was in crisis and how I should respond. Because I was not her minister or caregiver I could not easily progress through the model of intervention. I formulated a number of possible *plans* of action: go to the woman, stay where I am, talk to the young priest, or talk with the pastor. I also overheard what *plans* and *interventions* the young priest was formulating and imagined what the female pastoral associate was doing. In this situation there was *not* the opportunity for me to follow up, but I knew that the pastoral staff was following up by leading a memorial service for the child and family.

The *skills* I used were primarily assessment skills, determining *if* and *how* I should outwardly respond. I also called on the *attitudes and values* of crisis caring (see chapter 4). In particular I called on the attitudes of *respect* for the other ministers involved in the interaction; *caring* for the woman in crisis, accompanied with a desire to alleviate her pain; *prudence,* trying to make the wise choice of how to act; and remaining *non-anxious* as I was torn between listening to the pastor or the woman, and remembering the needs of my class. I also relied on the *values* of *faith,* that the helping and healing that would take place in this interaction would be companioned by God; *hope,* believing that this woman would get through this loss with or without me; and *competency,* remembering that pastoral ministers have lots of experience in dealing with crises such as these and trusting that their experience and education would provide them with the *competency* they needed.

3. Understanding the Crisis in a Broader Context

Background Information

The loss of a child is perhaps *the* most difficult loss a parent will ever face. The grief that results from this loss is intense and long lasting. It is an untimely loss that shatters our assumptive world and assaults our identity as parental caretakers.[1] In this case the loss may be further complicated by being a miscarriage or stillbirth, a socially unsanctioned, disenfranchised loss.[2] It is significant that the woman came *alone* to the rectory. We do not know *what* or *whom* she has for support at a time when additional support is particularly needed. This is a time when she may find other parents backing *away* from her as she is living their worst nightmare. Her hopes and dreams for the future have been altered and she may be experiencing an intrapsychic loss.[3] Grieving the death of a child is such a significant loss it will take a lifetime to grieve, and upsurges of grief[4] will occur at significant dates: birthdays, the day he would have entered school, received his learner's permit, or graduated from high school. She may experience *survivor guilt* (Rando 618) and may also believe that the child's death was preventable, two additional complicating factors.

In this encounter I was drawn to the young mother and thought I could help her because of my expertise in grief counseling and because I am a mother. The young woman appeared to still be in the first phase of grief—shock and disbelief—and was turning to the church for help. She was asking theological questions about baptism, memorial services, and appropriate Scripture readings. As I reflected on the encounter, I now believe that the best person to help her was the young priest who answered the door. He responded to her questions simply and directly, and appropriately referred her to another woman for conversation. He had no idea of who I was and this was *his* house.

Issues and Concerns for the Crisis Minister

My concern is, was I *right* in *not* answering the door and *not* speaking up? Did God put me in this situation because I was the right person to respond to Jane? Or did God put me in this situation to teach me patience, prudence, responsibility, and letting go?

4. Theological Reflection and Resources

In the preceding section, I already began to ask questions in theological terms. What was God asking of me in this situation? This for me is an issue of *discernment:* What is God desiring of me in *any* moment, and how do I know? In this encounter, I was *torn,* yet *not unsettled.* As difficult as it was for me *not* to walk down the stairs, after further prayer and reflection, I believe *this* is what God was asking of me at that moment and I feel at *peace* with my decision.

That night for the opening prayer for class I had chosen that day's lectionary Gospel reading so I was familiar with the reading from Mark that the young woman referenced. Reading it in class that night took on new meaning as I related to the class what had happened to me in the rectory. The reading is from Mark 5:21-43 and consists of two healing stories. The one is the healing of the woman with a flow of blood; the other is the healing of Jairus's daughter. In both cases, strong faith played a part in the healing. I wondered why the woman wanted that particular reading for a service. Did she find comfort in Christ's love? As I read the stories I wondered if she would think, "If only I had more faith, like those two, my child would not have died." Or would she feel comfort that Jesus could and would heal her pain from her loss? I hoped that if this reading were used in the service, she would not berate or blame herself for a lack of faith.

My theological orientation is toward *doing* good works (Matthew 25: 31–46). This encounter challenged me to consider alternative models of ministry: allowing others to minister, ministering through prayer (during and after), and reflecting on scriptural passages in which Jesus steps away from the crowds to pray and renew himself (such as Matthew 4:1 and 14:13; Luke 4:42 and 9:18) and when he empowers his disciples to minister (such as in Luke 9:1-6). There are many scriptural examples of empowerment, such as telling the disciples they had been given "the secret of the kingdom of God" (Mark 4:11).

What follows is totally from my imagination, as I never again spoke with the pastor (P), the young priest (YP), or the female pastoral associate (FPA).

1. What Might Have Happened (The Young Priest's Perspective): Description of Event

Vignette

A few months ago I was relaxing in the rectory reading the paper after a difficult day at work. Every few minutes I heard the doorbell ring and I ran down to the front door to let in a parishioner who was there for a finance meeting. About the fifth time this happened, I opened the door to see a woman (Caucasian, forties, with a briefcase) whom I had never seen before. She told me that she had come to teach a class. I invited her in and went to check the schedule, wondering if there might be a scheduling conflict. I checked the room schedule and there was indeed a scheduling conflict; there was no room for her in the rectory. I went to get the pastor, who was in the rectory for the meeting, and returned with him to the professor. She looked uncomfortable.

P = Professor

DM = Distressed Mother

M = Mark (Me)

MT = My Thoughts

P1: The doorbell rang when you were away. I wasn't sure if I should answer it or not.

M1: That's okay. This is Father Jim. He will help you with the room conflict and I will go and get the front door.

I leave the professor and Father Jim at the top of the stairs and go to answer the door.

DM1: Can you help me, please?

MT1: (It's supposed to be my day off. Why didn't I let Father Jim answer the door and I could have helped the professor?)

M2: What can I do for you? (*I manage a polite, albeit lukewarm invitation.*)

DM2: My baby has just died, and it is so hard!

MT2: (Good Lord, why me? What can I say to her? Why can't I be at the top of the stairs?)

M3: Won't you come in?

MT3: (She looks so upset; my heart goes out to her. At least I can invite her in.)

DM3: Yes, Father.

MT4: (She doesn't know that I am just a seminarian, that I'm not ordained yet, that I am not equipped to deal with this. But that seems so cold! Let's see what happens.)

DM4: Should I have had the baby baptized? He was dead when he was born.

MT5: (Ah, I think I can help. We just learned about this!)

M4: No, that was not necessary. We believe that the child is with God.

MT6: (Is that what the church teaches? I think so. Anyway, it sounds good and she looks a little less worried.)

DM5: Should I name him?

M5: That's up to you. You may find it helpful.

MT7: (I can do this. She is asking stuff I know.)

DM6: It's so hard (*crying*).

MT8: (Oh, no! Tears!)

DM7: Can I have a service?

MT9: (Phew, back to questions I can answer.)

M6: Yes, that is possible.

DM8: Could I have a reading from today's Gospel? It's something from Mark, but I don't remember what.

M7: We can check on it. I will get the lectionary and we can look it up.

I leave for a moment to get the lectionary and overhear the professor and Father Jim talking. Father Jim is telling the professor how much he liked her recent book on difficult deaths.

MT10: (So there is a grief expert here and I am the one to answer the door!)

DM and I spend a few moments looking at the Gospel reading. I suggest she sit with our pastoral associate who is here tonight and begin to plan a service. She thanks me and I go back to my office.

My Role

I am a seminary student spending time at the parish as part of my priestly training. In this instance I am priest and counselor to one of my parishioners.

2. Assessment, Analysis, and Response

— Subjective: identification of feelings evoked

— Objective analysis: identification of type of crisis, skills used, and model followed

Subjective Analysis

Feelings Evoked

I felt a variety of feelings. At first when I answered the doorbell for the professor, I was a bit *annoyed* to have to get up again and then *surprised* because I didn't know there was a class scheduled for that night. When I went to check on the conflict, I felt *confused* because I thought there was only one activity for the evening. On my way to Father Jim, I felt a bit *anxious* because he had made it clear that I was in charge and he wanted to be left alone. I was *relieved* when he said he would deal with the professor. When I went back to the professor and she told me the doorbell had rung again, I felt *confident* again as I was expecting another person from the finance committee. During my conversation with the Distressed Mother, I felt a myriad of feelings ranging from *sadness, distress,* and *insecurity* to *confidence, peacefulness,* and *surrender.*

Objective Analysis

Type of Crisis

I had never taken a crisis-counseling course before, but I have taken the basic pastoral counseling course in which we talked about **unanticipated crises,** and I remember thinking that the sudden death of a child certainly fits this category. I also thought of the grief counseling class I took and thought that this woman must be in extreme *shock* — the first phase of grief.

Model and Skills: ABC

From my introduction to pastoral counseling class, I remembered a model we had learned called **ABC** — Achieve Contact, Boil the Problem Down to Its Basics, and Cope Actively. I tried to keep that in my mind as she talked, but things went so fast, it was really hard. As far as skills are concerned, I would assess my responses as follows:

M1 — Information Sharing
M2 — Open Probe
M3 — Information Question
M4 — Information Sharing
M5 — Information Sharing
M6 — Information Sharing
M7 — Information Sharing

My understanding of crisis counseling is that the crisis counselor uses the skill of Information Questions a lot. In this case, the Distressed Mother was quite talkative and asked *me* a lot of questions so I think giving Information Responses was appropriate. As I look back, though, I wonder if I conveyed to her my sympathy and sadness at hearing of the death of her child.

3. Understanding the Crisis in a Broader Context

Background Information

Since this encounter I have discovered that the professor at the top of the stairs not only teaches a course on grief, and on crisis counseling, but has published books in *both* areas! I will write of the issues that this evoked for me in my next section. I actually used her book *Complicated Losses, Difficult Deaths* to see what information I could find on the death of a child. DM's child was actually a stillbirth, which would fall under the category of a socially unrecognized loss, or a *disenfranchised loss.* With a disenfranchised loss, the griever needs to have her loss acknowledged, recognized, and ritualized. Now her questions—about naming, baptism, and a memorial service—take on new meaning. Her loss is also the *death of a child* that falls under the list of deaths that are difficult due to the nature of the death. Other deaths that are difficult in and of themselves include sudden, traumatic, lingering, or violent deaths[5]—and this is before we look at additional complicating factors.

When parents experience the death of a child, their world is forever changed. Parental relationships are affected (Rando 620–622). As I look back, I wonder, where was her husband or the father of the child? Why wasn't he there with her?

Now that I have done some reading on crisis models, I see that ABC is one of the models suggested, so I was on target there.

Issues and Concerns for the Crisis Minister

I am left with a number of questions about myself in ministry. I have reflected a lot on whether I was the right person to help Jane. How could I, a single, unmarried man, with no children, understand a mother's pain of losing a child? What about future ministry situations? Can I do marital counseling? What about other women's issues like pregnancy, rape, menopause, or breast cancer? How can I adequately respond to women in these situations?

I am also left wondering if I was deceptive in not letting her know I was only a seminarian. Was this unethical?

Finally, I am left to wonder about my style in ministry. Do I prefer to give answers and not show feelings? Do I come across as knowledgeable and helpful or unfeeling and remote?

4. Theological Reflection and Resources

The passage from the Gospel of Mark became the starting point for me as I brought this situation to reflection and prayer. I sat with our pastoral associate and talked about this reading as she prepared the memorial service homily. She shared with me that the mother wanted the reading from Mark because it spoke to her that faith will see you through difficult times and may produce wondrous and unexpected miracles. We were both touched with what a positive spin the mother placed on that reading. I like to think she was also inspired by the first reading that day from the letter to the Hebrews (12:1–4), which speaks of the cloud of witnesses that surrounds us and encourages us to persevere and keep our eyes on Jesus. I am not sure I would have focused on my faith in Jesus at that point; I think I would have been more likely to rail at God.

I also have searched out theological information to see if I responded correctly to the baptism and naming question. The introduction to the *Rite of Baptism for Children* clearly states that we are to baptize a child who is in danger of death (III:8.1, IV:21.1). The woman's child was born dead, so there was no need to baptize the child. Sacraments are for the living. All canons referring to baptism of children assume a *living* child. Even canon 871 calls for the baptism of an aborted fetus only if the fetus is living (*Code of Canon Law*). The naming question is not a theological one as a child is given a name at birth, rather than at the time of baptism. Since the child was never alive he does not *have* to be named, but this would probably help the parents in their grieving process.

Finally, this encounter has forced me to reconsider the role of women in ministry. Until this encounter, I considered my gender to be an asset because I do not support the ordination of women and have only recently come to terms with women in lay ministry. This encounter opened my eyes to seeing how important it is to have a woman to provide ministry, and I found this in Sue, our pastoral associate. I first thought maybe the female professor (expert on grief) was placed there by God at that very moment to provide Jane with the needed resource. But as I prayed about it, I realized that two things happened in the encounter: (1) I was able to help the woman in what I knew best by appropriately responding to her questions. I think my answers had weight as I clearly represented the church to her and she desperately needed church support. (2) God gave me the wisdom to see that I needed to hand her over to a *female minister* who could respond to her as a woman, a mother, and as a liturgist trained to plan memorial services. In the end Sue and I co-led the memorial service and she preached the homily.

Some Final Reflections (by Roslyn)

The encounter I wrote about happened in some form and I am obviously the professor. Although the young priest's reflection is fiction, I think we can see that each person in this encounter was affected by what happened and the case could have been written by any of us. What was evoked, what issues emerged, what skills were used, and what theological reflection resulted would be different for each person involved. Writing this has helped me to come to terms with my judgment of the young priest and to be even more at peace with my decision not to answer the door. For me, the final theological lesson was to let go and let others minister so that God's healing presence would be made manifest in someone other than me — a humbling experience!

8

Violence

In the following case, the pastoral caregiver is a pastoral associate from the family's church. The case is written in the first person from her perspective.

1. Description of Event

Vignette

As part of my duties as a pastoral associate, I am on call for emergencies one weekend a month. In the year I have been with the church, I have received only a handful of calls while on weekend duty, and none of them really constituted pastoral *emergencies*. I have learned to keep the cell phone on, but not to expect that it will ring much—if at all. It was Memorial Day weekend and I was on call. I planned on staying near home just in case anything came up. It was Monday, Memorial Day, around midnight, and I was already asleep when I was awakened by a persistent ringing. Disoriented, I reached for the alarm and banged it, only to hear the ringing continue. I realized it was the church cell phone. I sat straight up and reached for the phone.

N = Nancy (me)

B = Brian, one of my parishioners

N1: Hello, this is Nancy Jones, pastoral associate of St. Anne's, may I help you?

B1: Nancy, is that you? Oh, Nancy, oh, God, Nancy.

N2: Yes, this is Nancy. Who is this?

B2: Nancy, this is Brian McGinn, from the church. I called the office and the answering machine said to call this number. Oh, Nancy, I can't believe she's been shot!

N3: Brian, I am here for you. Slow down a bit. Who was shot?

B3: It's Jackie, our beloved Jackie (*sobbing*) …

N4: (*I quickly try to place this family in my mind. I recognize the name and can envision the McGinn family: mother, Jackie; father, Brian; and three teenagers, Jared, Sarah, and Katie. They come to church every Sunday, and the teens are part of our youth group.*) Brian, what happened?

B4: We just got a call. Jackie was at a friend's house and someone broke in with a gun, and oh, Nancy, she was shot.

N5: Brian, where are you?

B5: I am on my way to the hospital—St. Paul's. Nancy, I don't know what to do.

N6: Brian, are you in the car? Is anyone with you?

B6: I am in the car almost at the hospital. I'm alone. Everyone else is at the cottage. They don't even know yet.

N7: Brian, are you able to drive the rest of the way?

B7: Yes. The hospital is right down the street.

N8: Brian, I am about five minutes from the hospital. I will meet you there in ten minutes.

B8: Okay.

I am now wide-awake. Within ten minutes I am in the emergency room of St. Paul's looking for Brian. I identify myself to the clerk, and she escorts me to a waiting room where Brian is pacing up and down. I wait with him to hear from the attending doctor.

This was the opening encounter of a pastoral emergency situation that has continued throughout the last month. Jackie had indeed been shot and died, murdered by someone who broke into her friend's house. Jackie was in the kitchen when the intruder broke in, and she probably turned when she heard a noise. As far as anyone can figure, she was shot immediately and the intruder took off. To date, no one has been arrested for this crime.

I was with Brian when he received the news from the doctor that Jackie had died from a shot to her head. I sat with him as he called his family and waited with him for their arrival. Over the next few weeks I have been with the family for the memorial service and for numerous phone calls and pastoral visits as they try to come to terms with Jackie's death.

My Role

I am the pastoral associate of a large, Roman Catholic, suburban church. In this situation I became more like *the pastor* being in charge of and responsible for *all* the pastoral needs of the family.

2. Assessment, Analysis, and Response

— Subjective: identification of feelings evoked

— Objective: identification of type of crisis, skills used, and model followed

Subjective Analysis

Feelings Evoked

The feelings I experienced during the first pastoral encounter included *shock, sadness, distress,* and *disbelief*—many of the feelings I imagine the family was experiencing. I also felt *thankful* that it was not *my* loved one who was shot, and then I felt *guilty* for feeling *thankful.* I even felt *angry – angry* that I was on call and not the priest, and *angry* at God for allowing this to happen. Even though I did not believe that God *caused* Jackie to be shot, I felt *angry* nonetheless. I also felt *empty*—almost devoid of all feelings—as I sat in the hospital with Brian.

Over the last month as I have ministered to the family, I have felt all those emotions and more. I have also felt *sad* and *upset* and *overwhelmed,* as well as *loved, relieved,* and *peaceful.* My emotions have run such a gamut, it is a bit disorienting.

Objective Analysis

Type of Crisis

This was a **situational crisis** that was also a *complicated loss and difficult death*. In the initial pastoral encounter, I responded to the *situational crisis;* as the month has progressed, I have ministered to a family in the first phase of *complicated grief.*

Model and Skills: CARING with Alex, ABCX with Family

Connect — I didn't have much time to make an initial connection as I was half-asleep when I answered the phone, but I answered the phone trying to sound as though I was available to whoever was calling (N1); as soon as I heard Brian's voice I was immediately alert and continued to focus on him and connect in N2 and N3.

Skill: Presence (N1, N2, N3)

Assess — By the end of N3, I am already beginning to assess what has happened, and get Brian to back up so that together we can assess and understand what happened. Brian's response in B4 that Jackie has been shot alerts me to the seriousness of the situation. The rest of the conversation up to N7 contains elements of Assessment. I am trying to assess if Brian is able to function, his state of mind, where he is, and if anyone is with him.

Skills: Assessment, Empathy, Probes, Information Questions

- N3, N4, N5, N6, and N7 are Probes and Information Questions asked to assess.

- Empathy is not overtly expressed, but it is implied in my trying to understand what has happened and how Brian is feeling, from his perspective.

Respond — My response is made through my Assessing Questions and then in my assurance that I am on my way (N8).

Intervene — The intervention actually happened as the conversation continued in the hospital.

Skills: Information Sharing, Self-Disclosure, Immediacy

- I was able to give the family Information about a funeral home, services, and bereavement resources.

— I Self-Disclosed my own sadness.

— I do not remember using Immediacy.

Network — At the hospital I was able to Network with healthcare providers and the chaplain on call to provide information and care for the family as they gathered. As my ministry with the family has continued, I have been able to share with them some resources about a support group and have referred them to a grief therapist.

Skills: Information Sharing, Referral

— This was not done in the phone conversation but did occur at the hospital and throughout the last month.

Get Together — This was mentioned specifically in N8, and then at the end of every visit we have, I set up a specific time to call or visit to follow up with the family.

Summary of Skills Used

N1 — Information Sharing, Open Probe
N2 — Information Sharing, Information Question
N3 — Information Sharing, Information Question, Assessment
N4 — Open Probe (Assessment)
N5 — Information Question (Assessment)
N6 — Information Question (Assessment)
N7 — Information Question
N8 — Information Sharing

In the hospital — Self-Disclosure, Information Sharing, Referral

Although my initial conversation was with Brian (individual), other conversations occurred with the entire family present.

Double ABCX Model (McCubbin and Patterson): See page 32 for a review of this model. Particular emphasis was given to the bB Factor, the adaptive resources of the family, and the cC Factor, the meaning that the family struggled to find in Jackie's death. The cC Factor will be addressed in section 4, Theological Reflection and Resources.

3. Understanding the Crisis in a Broader Context

Background Information

The McGinn family experienced the sudden and violent death of their mother and wife. Death by *homicide*[1] carries with it a number of complicating factors (Rando 540), including suddenness, trauma, violence, preventability, guilt, anger, a tendency for survivors to blame themselves, randomness, and secondary victimization.[2] Particular complicating factors for the McGinn family included:

— feeling **guilty** for not being there when Jackie was shot

— thinking, "If only she had come with us to the cottage." (**preventability**)

— thinking, "If only we had been there, her death could have been averted." (**self-blame**)

— struggling to understand **why** it was **our** mom and wife who had to die (**randomness**)

— coping with the image of their mother and wife's death as **violent** and **traumatic**

As I write this, Jackie's killer has not yet been found, and this also adds to the family's grief.

Statistics

Three out of five murders are actually committed by someone known to the victim, such as a relative, neighbor, or friend. Men are most often the killer and the victim. Ninety percent of homicides are committed by killers of the same race. In this case, since the murderer has not yet been found, we do not know if these statistics are true for Jackie. We are at most risk to be a homicide victim between the ages of twenty-five and forty-four. Jackie was forty-two. Homicides are most common in large cities. Jackie lived in a suburb of a large city. Handguns are the most common weapons. (Kastenbaum 209–210). Jackie fit some of these statistics, but other factors are not known.

Grief after a homicide will be more *intense* and *prolonged* (Rando 538). Survivors may experience repetitive thoughts, nightmares, rage, terror, depression, and numbness; they may experience sleep disturbances, headaches, and increased heart rates; or they may exhibit self-protective behaviors, change family roles, and feel a desire to search for the killer (Rando 539–540). Knowing that these feelings, symptoms, and behaviors may occur is helpful to the family and to the pastoral caregiver.

Homicide is classified as a complicated loss and difficult death because of its suddenness, violence, and unexpectedness (Rando 7–10; Walsh and McGoldrick 13–18; Karaban, *Complicated* 65–68). Difficult deaths can evoke extreme reactions in the pastoral caregiver as well as in the survivors.

Issues and Concerns for the Crisis Minister

I am left with the troublesome thought that if this could happen to the McGinn family, it could happen to me and my family.[3] This thought makes me want to *distance* myself from the McGinns, which is not a very helpful stance for the caregiver. How do I move *toward them* when my instinct is to *move away*?

The McGinns are struggling to find *purpose* and *meaning* in this death. I am also struggling to find purpose and meaning. How do I help them when I am struggling with some of the same questions and concerns?

4. Theological Reflection and Resources

Jackie's death and my ministry with her family have affected me more than any situation I have had to deal with since going into professional ministry. This is understandable on a *psychological* level, given the randomness and violence of the act. However, it is on a *theological* level that this death has most affected me.

I have certainly questioned God before asking questions such as: Why is there so much suffering in the world? Why do young children have to die, or suffer abuse, or go hungry? How can human beings be so hateful to each other? But these questions have been abstract, philosophical, almost academic conversations with God. Since I have not experienced any traumatic deaths, I have never questioned God on a *personal* level. Why *me*? Why *my* mom? Why *my* family? Although Jackie was not *my* mom, as I sit with the

McGinn family and *they* ask these questions, I identify with their spiritual angst and find that I have no good answers for them. *My* belief that God does not *cause* pain, suffering, and death does not *address their* pain. I put myself in their place and wonder what I would think of God if it *were my* mom. This causes me such discomfort that while I am sitting with them, I want to leave. I have to force myself to call and visit, and I feel inadequate and incompetent in my role as minister.

I know that this will not be my most difficult pastoral death and that I will have to come to terms with my discomfort and questioning if I want to stay in ministry. I also know that someday I will face a difficult, personal death and may ask the same questions that the McGinns are asking. I am even questioning whether I should be in professional ministry. Perhaps I don't have strong enough beliefs in God's love and goodness to provide leadership and guidance to others. Perhaps I don't have enough personal experience with pain, and death, to help others with their pain.

As I struggled with my own faith and vocation issues and was at a point of resigning from my position with the church, the youngest daughter, Katie, called me and said she had to see me right away. I reluctantly agreed to meet her at her house and steeled myself for another difficult visit of tears and anger. Instead, when I met Katie at the door, she was smiling and looked happier than I had seen her in weeks. I couldn't imagine what could have happened. She explained to me that as she was going though some letters and papers, she had found a letter from her mother, and wanted to share it with me. With her permission,[4] I include the letter as part of this reflection. We later shared the letter with the rest of the family and read the letter at Jackie's grave on the two-month anniversary of her death.

> My dear family,
>
> I do not know exactly what compels me to sit down tonight after you have all gone to bed and write this letter to you. But I am following some inner urge, some need, to put what I am feeling into words. As a woman of faith, I would say that I am responding to God speaking to me and nudging me to write what is in my heart. So, as strange as it feels to be writing this letter to you, I am feeling more at peace with each word I write.
>
> I have never shared this with anyone, and I imagine that if you are reading this, it is because I have died. I know that this will be very

difficult for you and I hope that you can help each other to get through the pain of my death. Please know that I loved you all and that I know you all loved me. If any of us argued or were at odds at the time of my death, please know that I died feeling only your love, not your anger. I somehow know this is what it will be like. What I have never told anyone is that I have known from a very young age that I would die suddenly and before my children were grown. I do not know how I know this, but I have come to terms with it and have accepted it as part of God's plan for me. I have not told any of you because I did not want to frighten or alarm you and I did not know *when* it would happen. But knowing this has allowed me to treasure each day with each one of you, and to see each day as a gift from God.

Please know that I have no fear of death. I truly believe that at death I will be united with God and will experience the joys of everlasting life. I also believe that I will then be there to greet each one of you when you cross over into eternal life. My concern is for all of you because you will question God for taking me from you. You need to know that it is my belief that God does not cause our death, but helps us through our physical death to spiritual life. In my case God has prepared me for this for many years, and this has helped me to live my life to its fullest — with no regrets.

I do not know how I will die, but if it is the result of a car accident from a drunk driver, please find it in your hearts not to pursue the driver of the other car seeking revenge. Please find it in your hearts to forgive that person and to get that person help with their drinking. If I die from a heart attack, please know that there is nothing more that you could have done. Do not second-guess why this or that was not detected. Sometimes hearts just stop beating and I accept that this may be my way to die. If I die as the result of a violent crime, I know this will be the hardest for you. But as you know, I am against the death penalty — even if I die a horrible and mutilating death. I ask that you let the court know that it is my desire that my killer not be put to death, but be imprisoned. I hope you can honor my wishes and not fill your hearts with hatred and revenge.

It is strange to write this letter. Part of me hopes that I may find it when I am 80, read it and laugh. But somehow, I know that will not happen. And so I thank God once again that I felt compelled to write this, because I know you will find some comfort in reading this after my death. Know that I died, and lived, loving God, and all of you, and I hope that you will be able to feel and rejoice in God's love and your love for one another. I will always be part of you and will be waiting for all of you when you join me in heaven.

Love,
Jackie/Mom

As Katie read this letter to me, I felt that God had given *me* a gift—a way of renewing my faith, of allowing me to know that even in traumatic and violent deaths, God is with us. Most of the time we will not find a letter like Jackie's and so our faith will be shaken. But Jackie's letter is a reminder to me that God does indeed send us signs and people throughout our lives and at the moment of our deaths to accompany us on our journey. As survivors and as pastoral ministers, we may not always have personal letters to attest to this, but it does not mean that the person who died did not know God's love or is not in heaven with God. I remember something my mother told me about death long ago. She said that death is always hardest on those left behind. I thought it an odd statement because I thought death must be hardest on the person who dies! But Jackie's letter has put death in a different light for me. Jackie wrote this letter to her family, not to me. But I believe that God also had her write this letter for me, to help bolster *my* faith and to help me with my own personal vocational crisis.

I know that I will continue to question my abilities as a pastoral minister, but I know I will also remember to look for other signs that God sends me to let me know that God is with me in my pain and doubt and discomfort.

Here is the brief service we did at Jackie's grave:

A Memorial Service for Jackie, on the Two-Month Anniversary of Her Death

Leader: We gather here today to remember our wife, mother, and friend, Jackie, who died so suddenly two months ago today. At the time of her death, we were so in shock that we are unable to remember much of what we said and did at her funeral. We wish today to express where we are now, and to offer prayers and remembrances. We call upon God, Our Creator, Sustainer, and Comforter, to be with us today.

We remember Jackie as a woman of great faith. We honor her

faith by the reading of her favorite Scripture passage, which has taken on new meaning for us.

Jared: (from Hebrews 12:1–3)

> Therefore, since we are surrounded by so great a cloud of witnesses, let us also lay aside every weight and the sin that clings so closely, and let us run with perseverance the race that is set before us, looking to Jesus the pioneer and perfecter of our faith, who for the sake of the joy that was set before him endured the cross, disregarding its shame, and has taken his seat at the right hand of the throne of God. Consider him who endured such hostility against himself from sinners, so that you may not grow weary or lose heart.

Leader: We hear these words differently today knowing that Jackie has pointed us to this passage for comfort, and to help us with our pain and struggles. She gave us many gifts in life, and continues to help us to grieve her death, through the beautiful letter she has written us.

Katie reads the letter. Each person who wishes to speak responds to what he or she is now feeling.

Leader: We continue to mourn Jackie's death and continue to cry tears of sadness at her sudden passing. But we have been strengthened through her reminder to us that God is with us — in Scripture, in our lives, and through Jackie's life *and* death. We pray for *strength* to endure the pain of not having her with us, *openness* to hearing and feeling God in our grief, and *wisdom* that we may grow in faith and understanding. We honor her life and death by living the values she has taught us: faith, hope, love, and forgiveness. May God and Jackie continue to help us all. Amen.

9

Community Crisis

The following case happened in some form but has been changed significantly.

1. Description of Event

Vignette

I was sitting at my desk preparing for a class on counseling skills that I was to teach the next day. The phone rang, and the following conversation occurred:

R = Roslyn (professor of pastoral counseling)

C = Cathy (former student, now a pastoral associate)

R1: Hello.

C1: Dr. Karaban, is that you? I am so glad that you are in. This is Cathy D., one of your former students. Do you remember me?

R2: Of course, I do, Cathy. How are you?

C2: Oh, Dr. Karaban, I don't think you want to know, but I don't know who else to call.

R3: It's fine that you called me, Cathy. Please tell me what is wrong.

C3: Well, as you may know I am the pastoral associate at St. Martha's and have been here for three years now. I loved my job and I came here because the pastor, Father Tim, personally invited me to come. I really like the way he does ministry and was so impressed with the work the parish does. I have been so happy the last three years ... (*tears and a long silence*).

R3: Cathy, I am here. This sounds very painful.

C4: I still can't believe it. Everyone will know soon. I don't know what to do. I feel so betrayed.

R4: Cathy, go on. What happened?

C5: It is still hard for me to say it out loud. This morning I went to my office and heard Father Tim in his office making a lot of noise. Someone was with him and Father Tim kept saying he wouldn't leave. I went in to see what was happening and Father Tim told me he was being asked to leave because someone had charged him with sexual abuse. He told me it wasn't true, but that he needed to go. He told me that I would have to tell the staff this afternoon and that he would be back. I just can't believe this is happening.

The conversation continued as I helped Cathy plan what she would say to the staff and who could help her take over the leadership and find resources for herself and her community. Cathy remained in contact with me over the next few weeks as the allegations became public and her parish continued to try to come to terms with Father Tim's departure and the charges that had been made against him. There were actually multiple allegations made by numerous men, spanning many years. Cathy and the whole faith community were devastated.

My Role

I continued to be *one* of Cathy's support resources. She called me from time to time to update me and to ask for support, prayers, and resources. One week after the allegations became public, I was asked to come to a parish staff meeting as a *consultant* to help them deal with their feelings and to advise on how to minister to the community.

2. Assessment, Analysis, and Response

— Subjective: identification of feelings evoked

— Objective: identification of type of crisis, skills used, and model followed

Subjective Analysis

Feelings Evoked

In the initial phone conversation, I felt *concerned* for Cathy. I was *angry* that yet another case of alleged sexual abuse was affecting yet another community. I felt *compassion* for any possible victims in this situation, particularly the boys (now men) who had made the accusations. As I worked with the staff, I became internally *impatient* with their defense of Father Tim. I was *confused* by their denial of any possible wrongdoing. I eventually felt *ethically conflicted* because of information I gained in the process (more will be said about this). I felt *relieved* as my role became more peripheral as I referred the staff and community to other consultants.

Objective Analysis

Type of Crisis

This was a **situational crisis** that is also an *ambiguous loss.* This was also a **community crisis,** a significant loss experienced by an entire community. Although the reactions and feelings individually ran the gamut, the *crisis event* affected the entire worshiping community as a whole.

Model and Skills: CARING

I used the individual CARING model with Cathy, and the CARING for Communities model with the staff. For this analysis, I will focus on the additional elements of the community model that were used (see pages 33–34 for a review of the model).

Connect — Additional elements for community caring: connecting to the community as a whole.

Because my initial contact had been with Cathy as an *individual,* I had to shift my thinking and approach away from an individual model. When I went to the staff meeting, I went thinking of them as a *staff* in crisis, representatives of a larger community of faith in crisis. I realized that individuals would have different reactions and feelings, but that my focus would be on the community. The *skills* for this part of the model are using *teaching, preaching, worship,* and *prayer* to establish and build broader connections. I knew I would not be the one to do the teaching, preaching, worship, or prayer, but I would be the one to help remind the staff of these ministries and to help them find *resources* for doing them. I helped connect them with *counselors* trained in sexual abuse allegations and community crisis, *preaching resources,* and even *preachers* who could be available if they were unable to preach, and *worship aids.* I did take an active role in grounding our work in *prayer* and reminding them of the importance of continuing to ground their response in prayer—in the various manifestations this would take.

Assess — The guiding principle here is to keep the community crisis in mind while acknowledging the different individual reactions to the crisis. I was able to connect the staff with professionals who could help them as individuals so that they could help minister to the community as a whole. I helped them define the crisis event as Father Jim being accused and suddenly removed and that this was something they shared in *common* even though their feelings and reactions might be very *different.*

Respond — I encouraged continual resourcing of other professionals, reminding the staff that they were *part* of the worshiping community in crisis as well as *leaders* of the community. I, too, sought professional help for resources and eventually to help me through my *moral conflict* that emerged in the midst of my consultation (see Issues and Concerns for the Crisis Minister).

Intervene —Active intervention includes teaching, preaching, prayer, worship, and counseling. Because I was involved as a *consultant,* I became the *coordinator* of the staff who arranged programs, meetings, prayer services, and counseling support for the parish. My role here was to help provide *referrals* and *information* and to *remind* the staff that the pastoral care needed for the community would need to take place on many levels.

Network — This was a key element in my interactions with the staff. I needed to continually remind the staff that they too were in need of pastoral care. Part of that care came from meetings with me; part came from separate sessions set up for the staff. During these sessions, they had their own workshops, prayer services, or counseling sessions. The staff often felt *guilty* for not being able to take leadership. My role was to remind them that they were *part* of the worshiping community in crisis, as well as leaders of that community.

Get Together — I worked with the staff to build in follow-up sessions with consultants and counselors as the weeks went by, both for the community and for themselves. There was a reluctance to do this because they just wanted to have the problem over and Father Tim back. As more and more allegations came out and Father Tim's return seemed less likely, there was an acceptance that they would need follow-up care for some time to come.

3. Understanding the Crisis in a Broader Context

Background Information

General

Father Tim was the fifth priest accused of sexual abuse in the diocese within a three-month period. Although this sounded like a large number and was devastating to each affected parish, these numbers represented 2.5 percent of active priests in the diocese.[1] Since the 1990s, many books have been published on this phenomenon, and reported cases have surfaced around the world; but it wasn't until 2002 that a widespread panic emerged in the United States.[2] American Catholics struggled to come to terms with their image of the priesthood as well as with the actions of particular priests. Without ignoring the particularities of the crisis for St. Martha's parish, it might be helpful to look at some more *general* information about abuse and crisis.

It is hard to estimate how many priests may be sexual abusers. Richard Sipe, a well-known psychotherapist and former priest, has conducted extensive interviews for twenty-five years. His best estimates are that approximately 6 percent of priests abuse; 4 percent abuse teens and 2 percent abuse prepubertal children. That means that 94 percent of priests do *not* abuse (Robinson 3). This figure needs to be kept in mind.

Most of the priests accused of sexual molestation have been *hebephiles*, not *pedophiles*. Hebephiles are attracted to postpubertal boys, ages fourteen to seventeen, whereas pedophiles are attracted to prepubertal children, under thirteen. This does not make the abuse any more acceptable, but it does help to dispel the image of priests attacking and molesting *young children.*

When a crisis occurs, the person or community in crisis may *generalize* their experience. Because *my* priest is an abuser, *all* priests are abusers. This generalization adds to the distress of the person or community in crisis. This may happen in other crises such as death or divorce. In chapter 8 the pastoral associate *generalized* the shooting death of her parishioner; because this happened to the McGinn family, it could happen to *anyone.* Although this is true, it is not likely. This is also known as *catastrophising,* taking one incident or situation and imagining the worst possible results. This significantly *adds* to the anxiety of the person or community in crisis and needs to be addressed.

Particular

The staff and parishioners at St. Martha's needed to understand general information about clergy sexual abuse and crisis, but they also needed to understand information *particular* to their parish and their pastor. This is a pivotal piece in getting through the crisis and yet this is an area in which information is often withheld. The parishioners knew what Father Tim was *supposed* to have done by what they read in the paper. Since Father Tim was removed, they were unable to ask him directly, but they did hear that he had denied the charges (the conversation he had with the pastoral associate). Therefore, they had two conflicting possibilities. They also had their own *experience* of Father Tim as a loving, charismatic, prophetic leader. Some now *doubted* their experience and worried that they had trusted an abuser; others *trusted* their experience and rejected the possibility of Father Tim as an abuser because it could not coexist with their image and experience of him as a priest. The parishioners were also influenced by their understanding of American justice, that each person is innocent until proven guilty and that we all, especially priests, deserve to be given the benefit of the doubt.

In another situation in the diocese, the allegation against the priest consisted of one relationship, twenty-five years earlier, with a seventeen-year-old female parishioner. In the case of Father Tim, multiple allegations surfaced, spanning a ten-year period. Because so many different allegations arose, parishioners compared the possibilities. Father Joe had had one relationship, and she was young; maybe Father Tim's situation was similar. Parishioners needed to be reminded that each situation was unique.

Because they would never be privy to all the allegations and details, the congregation struggled with a *lack of information* and *conflicting information.* They also struggled with what they *wanted* the truth to be and the *possibility* that this was not so. A few weeks into the crisis, Father Tim publicly admitted to the abuse and asked for forgiveness. As painful and shocking as this was, this admission united the parish in defining the crisis and in coming to terms with their pain.

Issues and Concerns for the Crisis Minister

In the midst of my consultation with the staff at St. Martha's, one of my students came to me to tell me that he was one of Father Tim's victims. As the parish struggled with whether to believe the accusations or Father Tim, I now had personal testimony of Father Tim's abuse. My student had reported the abuse to all the proper authorities and was receiving counseling. I could not reveal his testimony to the staff or the community at St. Martha's, yet knowing of his experience, I felt conflicted. Therefore, I excused myself from consultation; I could no longer remain neutral as the staff vehemently defended Father Tim and proclaimed his innocence. I also had to seek consultation and counseling to work through my personal feelings and conflicts.

This was not the first time I had found myself in this position. As a counselor I am told things in confidence that contradict what may be known publicly. For instance, I may know that a prominent politician is secretly gay, or having an affair, which contradicts the public image he is projecting as a happily married, heterosexual man. There are instances when I must break confidentiality, such as when my client says she is suicidal or that he intends to harm another person. But in this case, my student had already reported the abuse.

As staff members insisted that Father Tim was innocent, I became *angry* at what I judged to be their *naive trust.* This internal *judgment* prevented me from helping them express and work through their feelings. Just as I reminded them that as a staff they needed to be ministered to, I had to remind myself that I *also* needed ministry, support, and counseling. This *replication* of experiences and feelings is actually known as *isomorphism*, a mirroring or repetition of patterns that occurs on a number of levels. Here, as consultant, I continually reminded the staff that they were also in crisis and needed care; this pattern was replicated when I was reminded, by my internal conflict, that I also needed care. In this case, I actually needed to refer the consultation to someone else.

4. Theological Reflection and Resources

I refer to my personal knowledge of Father Tim's abuse as a *moral conflict*. I knew that the victim I had spoken to had reported the abuse and that I was not *legally* or *ethically* bound to further report the abuse. Yet, personally hearing the pain of one *victim* prevented me from being able to help. I could no longer hear the staff deny Father Tim's guilt because I now had personal knowledge of his actions.

It is not that I think I do not need ministering to. Due to the deaths that have occurred in my family this year, I have taken a leave of absence from counseling as I come to terms with my own grief. I am good at recognizing this about myself. But in this situation, I had been hopeful that Father Tim *was* innocent and so could more easily hear the pleas that this be true. Once I knew it to be false, I lost patience with those who refused to even consider this possibility. Usually I am able to hold two contradictory images or thoughts together — for instance, knowing that one of my students is gay even though he presents himself to the class as heterosexual. I am able to keep his confidence without feeling morally conflicted. But in this situation the staff's support of Father Tim became intolerable. I had reached my limit.

Theologically, I have always been taught to hate the sin but love the sinner. I can counsel people who have done very hurtful and harmful things, including sexual abuse. Each person, each life, and each story is different. When asked if I can counsel abusers, adulterers, and murderers, I say yes. I need to hear each person's story and the reasons for their actions. I also need to hear if they own up to their actions (sins) and are ready to seek forgiveness. I realized that this is what bothered me most about Father Tim. He denied his actions, thus adding to the pain and confusion of his victims and his parishioners. I realized that my own limitation in counseling and ministering lies in working with those who fail to recognize their sinfulness, take accountability for their actions, and seek forgiveness and reconciliation. What has helped me most in my own personal theological reflection is the biblical story of the prodigal son (Luke 15:11–32).

In the story of the prodigal son, the younger son squanders his inheritance and returns home, begging forgiveness. He does not ask for more money or to be accepted as a son but to be treated as a hired hand (Lk 19b). It is this attitude of humility, an acceptance of sinful actions, an openness to penance, and a willingness to change that appeals to me. I imagine myself as the father (mother) saying, "Of course, my son, I forgive you!" But in this story the father accepts, embraces, and forgives the son without even hearing these words. While he is yet far off, the father runs to him with open arms, ready to forgive. This action reminds me of God's abounding love for each one of us regardless of our actions. I like to think of God as forgiving us when we humble ourselves, beg forgiveness, and change our sinful ways. But this story reminds me that our God is a God who loves and forgives us even *before* we ask because only God can look into our hearts and know who we are. I am like the older brother who feels angry that his father so easily forgives a son who has done so many wrongs. I have to remind myself that life is not a contest and that heaven is accessible to all.

Father Tim did eventually confess, repent, and ask forgiveness for his sins. But we do not know what was in his heart all these years and *when* he asked God for forgiveness.

This may sound odd, but sometimes God is more loving and forgiving than I want God to be. I like to believe that the more good I do, the more I am loved. I need only remind myself of the laborers in the vineyard who, coming early or late to work, were all paid equally (Matthew 20:1–16). God's generosity extends to all. God's justice is not human justice.

It is painful to be reminded how judgmental I can be. It is also painful to think that I want to limit whom God loves or forgives. But it is in recognizing this issue that I have come to appreciate a distinction between human and divine law, and human and divine love. Of course, Father Tim is accountable to human law and to the disdain of those whom he hurt. But he is also accountable to divine Law and Love. In the end, I think all of us will be thankful that God

is the Final Judge. God is more generous, loving, and merciful than
I am.

Notes

Chapter 1

1. When using the word *communities,* I am specifically referring to *faith communities* (congregations) and *not* the broader community (town, city) in which we live.

2. This reference to Dr. Lester's distinctions comes from his lecture at Brite Divinity School in 1993. Although this is not a published concept, I wish to give credit to Dr. Lester.

3. The three general phases of grief are shock and disbelief, disorganization and active grieving, and reorganization and reintegration. See Karaban, *Complicated Losses,* for a detailed explanation of the grieving process.

Chapter 2

1. Clebsch and Jaekle note that their definition of four functions builds on Seward Hiltner's definition of pastoral care as healing, sustaining, and guiding (89–172).

2. For a fuller history of pastoral care see Clebsch and Jaekle, Browning, Holifield, and Gerkin. See also the writings of Gregory the Great, whose sixth-century treatise, *Pastoral Care,* became a classic guide.

3. By using the terms *communities of faith* and *worshiping communities,* I wish to include both Jewish *and* Christian places of worship. However, this book is written from a *Christian,* particularly *Roman Catholic,* perspective, and the intended audience is primarily Christian. Therefore, such terms as *pastoral minister* and *church* reflect the expertise and experience of the author and the issues and concerns of Christian congregations.

4. I am indebted to Mitchell and Anderson (171), who first introduced me to these three questions, to Elie Wiesel's poignant story of God's presence (75–76), and to various writings in liberation theology.

Chapter 3

1. When speaking of these assessment questions, Hoff referred only to the individual. I have added *family or community.*

2. Crisis reactions often involve loss, and thus grief. Careful assessment needs to distinguish whether crisis caring or grief counseling is needed. Crisis caring will be appropriate *if a situational crisis exists,* and early on in the grieving process.

3. These questions may not work with a community that has not *come* for counseling. A better question for a community might be: Where or how do you see yourselves (as a community) today?

4. This is my reworking of Hoff's questions.

5. These are my additions to Hansell.

6. All models described that are not mine—individual and communal—are paraphrased and summarized, and reference is made in the text to the original author and description of the model.

Chapter 4

1. Egan (4th ed. 61–75) lists pragmatism, competence, and ethics as values.

2. See Karaban (*Complicated* 111–117) for skills used in grief ministry.

3. See Switzer (*Pastoral* 208–221) and Clinebell (310–322) for more elaborate guidelines on when to refer.

4. See Karl (1) for a further list on how to make a good referral.

5. The closest Egan skill is closed probes (121–129).

Chapter 5

1. In the Roman Catholic tradition, the message given after the reading of the Gospel is traditionally called the *homily;* in the Protestant tradition, this message is referred to as the *sermon.*

2. I am indebted to Deacon Tom Driscoll for sharing with me his notes and ideas for his course on crisis preaching. The outline is mine but is influenced by ideas from Bishop Ken Unterer, Patricia Parachini, and notes, outlines, and conversations with Deacon Tom Driscoll.

3. I am indebted to Geary for an explanation of the structure and intentions of the general intercessions.

Chapter 6

1. See Rando (522–534) and Karaban (*Complicated* 35–43) for more information on suicide as a difficult death and a complicated loss.

2. See Guideline #7 for grief ministers (Karaban, *Complicated* 110).

3. Data taken from two websites: http://www.infoline.org/Crisis/stats.asp and http://www.befrienders.org/suicide/statistics.htm.

4. See Rando and also Karaban, *Complicated,* for further information on different types of complicated losses resulting in complicated grieving.

Chapter 7

1. See Rando (618) for a description of how shattering this experience is.

2. See Doka (273–274) and R. Karaban (*Complicated* 33–35) for further explanation of disenfranchised grief.

3. See Mitchell and Anderson (35–46) for a schema of different types of losses. An intrapsychic loss is described as the loss of an image of ourselves—in this case, an image of self as mother.

4. Rando (64) describes these upsurges as STUG, subsequent temporary upsurges of grief.

5. See Rando (7–10), Walsh and McGoldrick (13–18), and Karaban (*Complicated* 7) for complete lists of complicated deaths.

Chapter 8

1. The word *homicide* is used to denote the death of a person at the hands of another person; if a court rules that the death was *intentional* and *unlawful,* it is called *murder.* All murders are homicides; *some* homicides are murders. Other distinctions include *justifiable homicide,* which is also called *self-defense,* and *negligent homicide,* when carelessness results in the death of another person (Kastenbaum 208).

2. Survivors feel *revictimized* by those they thought would be helpful.

3. As caregivers we need to watch our own reactions to the horror and randomness of the act; the caregiver thinks, "This could have been my loved one," and emotionally steps away from the survivors (Rando 552).

4. Since this is a made-up case, no permission is actually necessary.

Chapter 9

1. These statistics are made up but are in the range of actual figures.
2. See http://www.religioustolerance.org/clergy_sex8.htm.

Bibliography

Printed Works

Allen, R. *Preaching the Topical Sermon*. Louisville: Westminster/John Knox, 1992.

Browning, D. *The Moral Context of Pastoral Care*. Philadelphia: Westminster Press, 1976.

Brueggemann, W. "Foreword." In *Psalms of Lament*, by A. Weems, ix–xiv. Louisville: John Knox Press, 1995.

———. *The Message of the Psalms*. Minneapolis: Augsburg Publishing House, 1984.

———. "Preaching to Exiles." In *Exilic Preaching*, edited by E. Clarke, 9–41. Harrisburg, Pa.: Trinity Press International, 1998.

———. *The Prophetic Imagination*. Philadelphia: Westminster Press, 1978.

Caplan, G. *An Approach to Community Mental Health*. New York: Grune & Stratton, 1961.

———. *Principles of Preventive Psychiatry*. New York: Basic Books, 1964.

Clarke, T. "One Road to Peace: Tender Love, Firm Justice." *The Way* (1982): 175–183.

Clebsch, W., and C. Jaekle. *Pastoral Care in Historical Perspective*. New York: Harper & Row, 1964.

Clinebell, H. *Basic Types of Pastoral Care and Counseling*. Rev. ed. Nashville: Abingdon Press, 1984.

Code of Canon Law. Washington, D.C.: Canon Law Society of America, 1983.

Doka, K. "Recognizing Hidden Sorrows." In *The Path Ahead: Readings in Death and Dying*, edited by L. DeSpelder and A. Strickland, 271–280. Mountain View, Calif.: Mayfield Publishing Company, 1995.

Egan, G. *The Skilled Helper*, 7th ed. Pacific Grove, Calif.: Brooks/Cole, 2002. 4th ed. (1990).

Ellis, A. *Reason and Emotion in Psychotherapy.* New York: L. Stuart, 1962.

Festinger, L. *A Theory of Cognitive Dissonance.* Palo Alto, Calif.: Stanford University Press, 1957.

Geary, P. "Preparing the General Intercessions." *Music and Liturgy* 28:1 (Spring 2002): 9–13.

General Instruction of the Roman Missal. Washington, D.C.: U.S. Catholic Conference, 2003.

Gerkin, C. *An Introduction to Pastoral Care.* Nashville: Abingdon Press, 1997.

Hansell, N. *The Person in Distress.* New York: Human Sciences Press, 1976.

Hater, R. "Celebrating a Life Well Lived." *Ministry & Liturgy* 31, no. 3 (April 2004): 13–14.

Hermann, J. *Trauma and Recovery.* New York: Basic Books, 1992.

Hill, R. *Families under Stress.* New York: Harper & Row, 1949.

Hiltner, S. *Preface to Pastoral Theology.* Nashville: Abingdon Press, 1958.

Hoff, L. *Battered Women as Survivors.* London: Ruthledge, 1990.

———. *People in Crisis: Clinical and Public Health Perspectives.* 5th ed. San Francisco: Jossey-Bass, 2001. 4th ed. (1995).

Holifield, E. *A History of Pastoral Care in America: From Salvation to Self-Realization.* Nashville: Abingdon Press, 1983.

James, R., and B. Gilliland. *Crisis Intervention Strategies.* Belmont, Calif.: Wadsworth/Thomson Learning, 2001.

Jeter, J. *Crisis Preaching: Personal and Public.* Nashville: Abingdon Press, 1998.

Jones, W. "The A-B-C Method of Crisis Management." *Mental Hygiene* 32 (January 1968): 87–89.

Karaban, R. *Complicated Losses, Difficult Deaths: A Practical Guide for Ministering to Grievers.* San Jose, Calif.: Resource Publications, Inc., 2000.

———. "Isaiah 63:16–64:12: Pastoral Implications." *Lectionary Homiletics* 4 (1993): 29–30.

———. "Pastoral Care and Counseling: They're Not Just by Clergy Anymore." *SPCC Newsletter* 17 (July 1999): 1–3.

———. *Responding to God's Call: A Survival Guide.* San Jose, Calif.: Resource Publications, Inc., 1998.

Karl, J. "Guidelines for Making a Successful Referral." *SPCC Newsletter* 4 (October 1992): 1.

Kastenbaum, R. *Death, Society, and Human Experience*. 6th ed. Boston: Allyn & Bacon, 1998.

Lester, A. Lecture, Brite Divinity School, Fort Worth, Texas, June 24, 1993.

Lindemann, E. "Symptomatology and Management of Acute Grief." *American Journal of Psychiatry* 101, no. 2 (1944): 141–148.

Mawby, R., and S. Walklate. *Critical Victimology*. London: Sage, 1994.

Mayeroff, M. *On Caring*. New York: Harper, 1972.

McCubbin, H., and J. Patterson. "The Family Stress Process: The Double ABCX Model of Adjustment and Adaptation." *Marriage and Family Review* 6 (1983): 7–37.

McGee, T. "Some Basic Considerations in Crisis Intervention." *Community Mental Health Journal* 4 (1968): 319–325.

Mitchell, K., and H. Anderson. *All Our Losses, All Our Griefs: Resources for Pastoral Care*. Philadelphia: Westminster Press, 1983.

Mullen, P., and E. Hill. "A Family Systems Model for Pastoral Care and Counseling in Times of Crisis." *Journal of Pastoral Care* 44 (1990): 250–257.

New Revised Standard Version of the Holy Bible. New York: Oxford University Press, 1989.

Oates, W. *The Christian Pastor*. Philadelphia: Westminster Press, 1951.

———. *Pastoral Counseling*. Philadelphia: Westminster Press, 1974.

Oden, T. C. *Crisis Ministries*. New York: Crossroad, 1986.

Parachini, P. *Guide for Lay Preachers*. Chicago: Liturgy Training Publications, 2000.

Patton, J. *Pastoral Care in Context: An Introduction to Pastoral Care*. Louisville: Westminster/John Knox, 1993.

Premnath, D. *Eighth Century Prophets: A Social Analysis*. St. Louis: Chalice Press, 2003.

Puryear, D. A. *Helping People in Crisis*. San Francisco: Jossey-Bass, 1979.

Ramsey, L. "The Theology of Pastoral Preaching." *Quarterly Review* 22:2 (Summer 2002): 179–191.

Rando, T. *Treatment of Complicated Mourning.* Champaign, Ill.: Research Press, 1993.

Rite of Baptism for Children. Vol. 1 of *The Rites of the Catholic Church.* Collegeville, Minn.: Liturgical Press, 1990.

Robinson, B. A. "What Percentage of Priests Abuse, and Whom Do They Victimize?" http://www.religioustolerance.org/clergy_sex8.htm (April 25, 2005).

Rogers, C. *On Becoming a Person.* Boston: Houghton Mifflin, 1961.

Sipe, A. W. R. *Sex, Priests and Power: Anatomy of a Crisis.* Levittown, Pa.: Brunner/Mazel, 1995.

Slaikeu, K. A. *Crisis Intervention: A Handbook for Practice and Research.* 2nd ed. Needham Heights, Mass.: Allyn & Beacon, 1990.

Stone, H. *Crisis Counseling.* Rev. ed. Minneapolis: Fortress Press, 1993.

Switzer, D. "Crisis Intervention and Problem." In *Clinical Handbook of Pastoral Counseling,* edited by R. Wicks, R. Parsons, and D. Capps, 132–161. Mahwah, N.J.: Paulist Press, 1985.

———. *The Minister As Crisis Counselor.* Nashville: Abingdon Press, 1986.

———. *Pastoral Care Emergencies: Ministering to People in Crisis.* New York: Paulist Press, 1989.

Taylor, B. "Preaching into the Next Millennium." In *Exilic Preaching,* edited by E. Clarke, 91–100. Harrisburg, Pa.: Trinity Press International, 1998.

Unterer, K. *Preaching Better.* Mahwah, N.J.: Paulist Press, 1999.

Weaver, A., J. Preston, and L. Jerome. *Counseling Troubled Teens & Their Families: A Handbook for Pastors and Youth Workers.* Nashville: Abingdon Press, 1999.

Weems, A. *Psalms of Lament.* Louisville: Westminster/John Knox Press, 1999.

Wiesel, E. *Night.* New York: Avon, 1958.

Wimberly, E. P. *Pastoral Counseling and Spiritual Values: A Black Point of View.* Nashville: Abingdon Press, 1982.

Walsh, F., and M. McGoldrick. "Loss and the Family: A Systemic Perspective." In *Living Beyond Loss,* edited by F. Walsh and M. McGoldrick, 1–29. New York: W. W. Norton, 1991.

Online Publications

http://www.befrienders.org/suicide/statistics.htm

http://www.infoline.org/Crisis/stats.asp

http://www.religioustolerance.org/clergy_sex8.htm

Other Titles by Roslyn A. Karaban

RESPONDING TO GOD'S CALL
A Survival Guide

Paper, 144 pages, 5½" x 8½", ISBN: 0-89390-431-7

This is a book about discernment — tuning in and listening to God's call, prayerfully reflecting on that call, clarifying what that call is, and responding to what you feel and hear. People involved in all sorts of ministry, and those who would like to be involved but find their calling in discord with the position of the church, will find this book a valuable tool in determining what is of God and what is not, and how to set their own direction. The book includes a series of personal stories from the author and others to help illustrate the concepts. A unique feature of this process is that it can involve loss — the loss of who you are today in order to become what is your calling. Dr. Karaban carefully shows how this process of loss closely resembles the grieving process, and helps you mourn and move through the losses to become what God has called you to be.

COMPLICATED LOSSES, DIFFICULT DEATHS
A Practical Guide for Ministering to Grievers

Paper, 144 pages, 5½" x 8½", ISBN: 0-89390-476-7

Suicide, sudden losses, lingering illnesses, the death of a child, murders, miscarriages and other difficult deaths evoke grief symptoms and reactions that are more intense and last longer than ordinary grief. Such complicated losses are especially challenging for grief workers and may impact whole communities. This resource is intended for individual study or as a text for an advanced grief ministry course. It includes study questions, exercises, an extensive bibliography, and an index.

Reviews

"*Complicated Losses, Difficult Deaths* is a most complete and informative book on understanding different kinds of grief and ministering to those in grief. An absolute 'must read' for every minister, caregiver and professional in bereavement work."

— *J. Mark Ammerman, pastor, hospital chaplain and author of* Help During Grief

"Roslyn Karaban has written an eminently useful book for anyone involved in grief ministry. She has collected excellent resources to which she adds her own compassion, wisdom and pastoral experience. Together with engaging cases and study questions, this is a superb text for the seminary classroom as well as adult education courses in the church and synagogue."

— *Carroll Saussy, Howard Chandler Robbins professor of pastoral theology and care, Wesley Seminary, Washington, D.C.*

 Order these books from your local bookseller, or call 888-273-7782 (toll-free) or 408-286-8505, or visit www.resourcepublications.com

More for Grief Ministry

GRIEF MINISTRY
Helping Others Mourn

Donna Reilly Williams and JoAnn Sturzl

Paper, 195 pages, 5½" x 8½", ISBN: 0-89390-233-0

Grief Ministry: Helping Others Mourn fills the need for an up-to-date resource that combines spiritual and psychological insights about griefwork. It covers general aspects of grieving, empathy, communication, listening, and prayer. The authors share insights on handling difficult situations, including suicide, the death of a baby, job loss, AIDS, and divorce.

Reviews

"A wonderfully sensitive, compassionate, well-balanced overview of a complex subject that will bring information and inspiration to the grief experience."

— *Rabbi Dr. Earl A. Grollman, author of Living When a Loved One Has Died*

"For the helper who realizes that a desire to help is not enough, this practical book will be very welcome."

— *Nancy C. Reeves, PhD, registered psychologist, Island Loss Clinic, Victoria, British Columbia*

"*Grief Ministry* ... is comprehensive, while additionally detailed and focused. It will make a real contribution to the field of death and dying."

— *Linda E. Harper, bereavement coordinator, Kaiser Permanente Hospice Program, Norwalk, Calif.*

More for Grief Ministry

DREAMS THAT HELP YOU MOURN

Lois Hendricks

Foreword by Wayne E. Oates,

professor of psychiatry emeritus, University of Louisville

Paper, 176 pages, 5½" x 8½", ISBN: 0-89390-395-7

Author Lois Hendricks presents many examples of dreams — gleaned from personal interviews and from literature — to demonstrate how dreams serve a purpose. You'll learn that dreaming after the death of a loved one — whether a family member, friend, or pet — is normal; in fact, dreaming is the soul's way of mourning. This book will be a powerful comfort to the grieving and a useful referral book for counselors.

Reviews

"*Dreams That Help You Mourn* is simple and straightforward, unencumbered by dense scholarly theories and endless psychological analysis, but it is psychologically sound and, from a pastoral viewpoint, immensely insightful and wise. By its very richness, the collection of examples provides a strong argument for the importance of dreams in grief-work."

— *Richard Woods, OP, adjunct professor of theology, Black Friars at Loyola, Chicago*

"*Dreams That Help You Mourn* will be invaluable to those of us who counsel grieving people. Lois Hendricks has provided excellent insights in an easy-to-use format."

— *Bill Hoy, Premier Resource, Lakewood, Calif.*